OUT FROM UNDER

FOREWORD BY DOCTORS
J. RANEY, M. DILLWORTH, & S. QUICK
DAWN STEFANOWICZ

OUT FROM UNDER

The IMPACT *of* HOMOSEXUAL PARENTING

EDITED *by* HERMAN GOODDEN

ANNOTATION
PRESS
A Division of WinePress Publishing Group

Annotation Press (PO Box 428, Enumclaw, WA 98022) functions only as book publisher. As such, the ultimate design, content, editorial accuracy, and views expressed or implied in this work are those of the author.

ISBN 13: 978-1-59977-011-6
ISBN 10: 1-59977-011-3
Library of Congress Catalog Card Number: 2007929421

Printed in the United States.

Endorsements

O ut From Under: The Impact of Homosexual Parenting is a story of victimization and survival, the precious gifts of faith and hope, our universal need to forgive and be forgiven, and the triumph of true love.

Most are aware of the judicial and legislative attempts to redefine marriage as an institution unrelated to children. Hidden from the general public is a growing movement within psychiatry to normalize all paraphilias, including the sexual abuse of children. Some psychiatrists even claim that incest can be healthy. It is easy to see how these two movements will intersect. This is why the message of Out From Under is so critical now.

Dawn Stefanowicz's story bears witness to the devastation wrought upon children by sexual abuse and other elements inherent to the gay subculture. For this reason, Out From Under should be read by every legislator, lawyer, physician and mental health professional in a position to lobby for the best interests of children.

May society heed Dawn's courageous testimony and spare other innocents the suffering she and her siblings sustained. We must refuse to sacrifice our children on the altar of diversity.

Michelle A. Cretella, M.D.
Board of Directors, American College of Pediatricians
Chair, Committee on Sexuality, ACP, United States

Out From Under is a personal account told in an emotional narrative. Stefanowicz tells of the enormous burden that was thrust upon her as a young person, a burden that is too great for any child. This story compels one to ponder the vulnerability of children, human suffering, and the meaning of life itself.

Senator Anne Cools
Ottawa, Canada

Dawn Stefanowicz has the courage to write a politically incorrect book. She has the right because she was raised in a homosexual environment and suffered because of it. We need honest literature from all perspectives on this divisive topic – to date there are few books like this one, which argues that such environments are disturbing to children. There need to be many more books that tell it like it is.

Professor John Patrick, M.D.
Augustine College
Ottawa, Canada

Not amazingly, the best studies available show the multiple emotional and character problems of children, adolescents, and young adults who have grown up in a motherless or fatherless environment.

Dawn Stefanowicz writes...her personal experience, illustrating the unnaturalness of her parenting situation, the hypocrisy of those in her environment who pretended not to see this unnaturalness, and the loneliness of a child who is imprisoned in that situation.

After all, this girl was more natural and felt more normal than the others who did as if nothing was amiss. She had a terrible childhood, in all. Don't think that does not leave deep scars. And don't think her story stands alone. In several variations, it is the story of most of these children. I know them. They are forced to repress their most normal feelings and needs.

But she has performed a work of charity: warning, opening at least some eyes, moving at least some hearts to protect the most defenseless. That process mostly starts with a few isolated dissidents who have the courage and inner independence to speak out. Dawn will inspire others, no doubt.

Gerard J.M. van den Aardweg, Ph.D.
Psychologist, specializing in the treatment of homosexuality for over forty years
Author of many articles and several books on homosexuality, the Netherlands

Dedication

To the defense of innocent children
who cannot speak for themselves

Contents

Foreword

This book offers the reader a unique look into the "intriguing new world" of parenting by those involved in homosexual relationships. In her writing of this book, the author is courageously open about the various periods of her life and the troubling times she faced as a young girl, adolescent, and young adult. We learn how she dealt with her family and parental figures who influenced and dominated her life as they pursued their chosen ways of living. In *Out From Under,* we truly are privileged to see not only the good, but the bad and the ugly experiences of her family life as well. In this history of her upbringing and life, Dawn shares with us not only chronological accounts of her experiences, but also the emotional challenges and struggles she endured and conquered in becoming the person she is today. The premature death of her parental figures now has allowed Dawn to feel freer to share her story with the world, both to further her own psychological healing and to educate and inform the reader.

In an imperfect world, one would expect to see some problems in most households, regardless of whether the parents are involved in same- or opposite-sex relationships. Unfortunately, there are those who, with misguided political correctness, would like to silence any description of problems among those with homosexual relationships. Despite this, Dawn has had the courage to gift the reading public with her very personal life story, and so enhance our understanding of the kinds of challenges one might perhaps see in some of these newer forms of households.

And so, it is with great enthusiasm that we now recommend to the reader Dawn Stefanowicz's story. She provides us with descriptions and pictures of her life that go beyond mere facts and information, to a gripping account of her real life experience.

This Foreword and the Afterword were written by John Raney, M.D., Marc S. Dillworth, Ph.D., and Sharon Quick, M.D.

John Raney, M.D., is a forensic psychiatrist whose past work has involved a variety of settings including federal prison/jail, treatment settings for the seriously mentally impaired as well as managed care, mental disability assessments, and treatment of substance abuse and eating disorders. In addition, he has been involved in teaching and training programs and has a special interest in family structure as it impacts the raising of children. Marc S. Dillworth, Ph.D., is a licensed psychotherapist who specializes in the treatment of unwanted same-sex attraction, and gender identity disorder in children. Sharon Quick, M.D., is retired from pediatric anesthesiology and critical care. Her research interests include reference accuracy and children with parents involved in homosexuality.

Preface

The purpose in writing this book is to deliver an open, honest, and balanced account of what it was like growing up with a homosexual father and a weak, subservient mother. As a child, I struggled to deal with all the vivid and explicit sexual experiences, conflicts, and confusion I faced within this family setting.

As I have done research, I have come across individuals in North America who have publicly shared aspects of their personal stories of growing up with a same-sex attracted parent, and the difficulties that arose for them in that environment. What makes my story unique is that I am willing to share the full story—no holds barred.

However, in doing so, I want to confirm my lasting love for my biological father. I will always love him. He has gone on before me to a better place, and I miss him very much. There are many times when I wish we could get together for a chat, share a light-hearted laugh, do something fun, or just quietly sit together. Such times together did not happen often while he was on earth, as he was always engrossed in his business and extra-familial friendships. More than anything during my growing-up years, I just wanted him with us, providing strong, nurturing masculinity and a real sense of protection.

As my father, he modeled and taught me a strong work ethic and business sense, and he inculcated the sort of mature responsibility and endurance that make it possible to overcome adversity. Like any father, he was not always proficient or consistent in all of these things. Even so, at times through reverse education—showing me how not to behave—he bequeathed to me through difficult circumstances a courageous resolve to live life honorably and to the full. He set a high standard for me in his expectations of my career achievements. For this, I am truly thankful. Shifting as they were, he also shared his cultural values and his intellectual and moral philosophies with me. He was my dad and he will always be my father. In writing this book, my aim is not to hurt his name or reputation in any way. Rather, I would like to honor him, but still present a picture of our family life in an open and honest manner. I desire to share my own moments of joy as well as my struggles, pain, fear, and confusion in a manner that will broaden the reader's understanding of how parents and family can affect their children.

If there was a way to bring my father back, I would. I would not trade my father for any other. He did his best. I know that now. He did not intend to hurt me by his life choices or deny me the opportunity of being genuinely loved. But his ability to give his children the attention and affection they deserved was weakened by his own neediness and his restless search for a father type who would love, affirm, and attend to him. He wanted acceptance and a sense of belonging more than anything. He longed for and sought to obtain the sort of male companionship and love that he had never known as a child. But, as he sought to meet his own emotional needs through his gay lifestyle, the legitimate needs of his own children were often ignored. In recounting these incidents, I have had to forgive my father again and again to avoid becoming enmeshed in bitterness. I have written this book not out of spite, but with a desire to get out from under the wreckage created when sexual boundaries are obscured, to achieve freedom through telling the truth, and to benefit other children who have endured a similar household. It is quite possible my sharing may help them resolve their own issues.

During my growing-up years, there were far too many lies told as I hid my personal life from others and worried that I would offend not only my father but his partners and friends. I was concerned that my school friends and work mates would reject me if they knew about my father's numerous sexual partners and lifestyle. I have gone for years at a stretch telling hardly a soul about my deepest concerns and fears, and even now as I share my story, I feel a sense of guilt, like I am betraying my parents and siblings in exposing family secrets. But I have weighed the consequences of telling the truth against the higher purpose of shedding light on how parents and family structure can negatively impact children. In doing so, I hope to encourage the development of a society in which all children live safely in families in which their best interests and needs are secured for them. It has been said that the greatness of a society can be measured best in the care it takes in protecting those citizens who are least able to take care of themselves. Children, of course, are among this group. It is hoped that those who govern national policies will not allow the special interests of any group to trump the welfare or best interests of our children, who indeed represent the future of any society or nation.

My father ultimately revealed how he came from a very dysfunctional family where sexual boundaries were violated and incestuous relationships occurred. This dysfunction and trauma not only deeply affected his life, but also later the lives of his family and children. Despite all this, my father had a strong spiritual background that he shared with his children. Indeed, he was involved in church work when he was younger, and while for years he did not seem able or willing to follow biblical guidelines and admonitions in his own life, he did introduce his children to its teachings. Later as each family member struggled as best we could with the turmoil and confusion in our relationships and within our own lives, it was the faith and guidance provided by the Scriptures that helped me endure and even grow through these dark times in my life.

In writing about my life and family experiences, I have been governed by my best recollection of the people, circumstances, feelings, attitudes, motivations, observed consequences, and associated time frames. Some of my family members would have preferred that I not write or talk about any of my family experiences. Out of consideration for their concerns, names of individuals have been changed except where that person was a public figure. Also, while I've tried to communicate my experiences as gently and carefully as possible, I realize that the reader may not be comfortable with all aspects of my story. To be frank, some of the accounts are quite disturbing. However, if I am to be faithful to the truth, I'm afraid this is really unavoidable.

Preface

Achieving the ideal of heterosexual marriage in form only is no guarantee of health or wholesomeness. That I hope to expose the horrors of my upbringing while still elevating marriage as the primary haven for the procreation of children is not an indication of blindness, hypocrisy, or the passing on of blame. Rather, it is a sign of my conviction that there is a better way to live.

Certainly families and children matter. It is my hope that by sharing my experiences, readers in general, and those in position of influence and authority in particular, will be better informed and guided in making decisions that may affect profoundly our families and their children, who are the hope and future of the next generation.

Acknowledgments

There are so many dear family, friends, and associates who have encouraged me on this journey.

A tremendous thank you to

My husband for his fervent love and dedication to me and unflagging commitment toward the completion of the book;

My children for their bountiful joy, energy, and love;

My relatives who offered their trust, persistence, and hope;

My friends and prayer partners: Alice and Danny, Anne Marie and Mike, Barbara, Brenda, Carie and Leonard, Clara and Clair, Dawn, Debbie and Rien, Debbie N., Denise, Diane, Donna and Dan, Gail, Gisela and Jim, Gisele and Jack, Gwen, Helen and John, Jakii, Jan, Jane, Janice D., Jo-Ann, Kay, Kim and Pieter, Leslie and Les, Linda and Mark, Mal, Marlene, Mary and Dwight, Nancy and Gary, Onalee and Mike, Ruth, Susan and Geoffrey;

Janice G. for her timely assistance;

My editor, for his objective discernment, long hours, and precise recommendations to supply structure, improve the appearance, and tighten up the manuscript;

John Raney, M.D., Marc Dillworth, Ph.D., and Sharon Quick, M.D. for their unfailing support;

Others who, over the years, have by their examples enriched my life and borne witness of true forgiveness, gratitude, wholeness, and generosity.

Introduction

W ill you come with me to the end of the pier?" Dad asks. Ordinarily there is nothing I long for more than times alone with this man I too rarely get to be with. But tonight his question fills me with foreboding. The old wooden pier stretches out into the inky blue lake to a depth where the water that laps against its weathered posts is well over my head. I'm a pretty good swimmer, but even so, his request unnerves me. It would be one thing to walk out there with a father who loved me unconditionally and could be depended on to protect me, but more and more I am coming to understand that this is not the kind of father I have.

I am nine years old, and our family is staying for a week in mid August at the cottage of some friends. At least, I've been here all week with my mother and brothers. Mom's inside now, cleaning up after supper, and my brothers have run off into the woods to play. While Dad helped bring us all up here and he is here this last night of our holidays, most of this week he has been unwilling to stay with us. It hasn't been work that has called him away, but pleasure. The hard truth that all of us struggle to understand is that Dad prefers the company of other men to that of his wife and children. A few of the transitory and violent relationships he has had with these men have ended in their suicides. Though I cannot help but love him, I am starting to see that my father is a very dangerous man. If he can behave so abominably toward those men he professes to love, then what might he do to those he does not love, like us?

"Dawn, will you come with me to the end of the pier?" he asks again. "So I can get a picture?" I hadn't noticed the camera before. This calms some of my fear but not all of it. We proceed along the boardwalk of sun-bleached boards, and about three-quarters of the way out he stops and waves me out to the very end. Out this far the boards don't feel as solid as I'd like, but I want to please him and so I go out to perch on the very last one and turn around to face him. "That's fine; stay there," he calls, framing the shot as I gingerly kneel down on one knee, holding the front paws of our Chihuahua, Skipper, who—just as nervous as I am—carefully balances on his hind legs. The picture taken, Dad immediately and wordlessly turns and walks away, leaving me alone and afraid in this precarious place to which he's invited me. This is the story of my life.

The Fruit of Deception

My parents, both from large farming families, were married in 1960 on a warm summer's day, surrounded by family and friends in the small town of Belleville, Ontario. My mother, Judith, at twenty-six, wore a simple white wedding dress with a V-neckline covered in lace. She appeared happy in their few wedding pictures, standing next to this clean-cut younger man, Frank, who had just turned twenty. She had recently turned down the advances of two men—her physician and a Spanish man who had lavished her with gifts of ruby costume jewelry—because neither of them shared her United Pentecostal faith.

Religiously, both my parents had been raised in small country Protestant churches, with my father transferring during his teens from a Salvation Army chapel to my mother's particular sect of the Pentecostal denomination. Growing up, my mother attended church regularly, conforming to the church's outward code of conduct, while my father sought a church that endorsed a more rigorously strict legalism. I believe they could have been compatible religiously if they'd taken the time to explore and develop their understanding of the faith. But instead, they merely sought rules to govern their lives without having any understanding of love and grace.

Neither of my parents saw much to emulate in the marriage relationships of their parents. Though both of my grandparents' marriages remained intact, they were at best grim truces riddled with pain, deception, and profound disappointment that none of the partners believed could ever be fixed. The festering perversions unleashed in my father's family set the stage for enormous problems in the next generation. My father and all of his siblings were sexually wounded to one degree or another.

My mother's negative legacy had more to do with a lack of attention or affection rather than a surfeit of the wrong kind. She longed for security and certainty. At one point in my mother's young life, during the Depression era, she hid under the kitchen table as a wealthy couple came to look at her, with the intention of possibly adopting her. Once she was dragged out into the open and her prospective parents saw her, they rejected her outright, openly commenting on how ugly she was.

My parents' courtship had been short. They first met in a small church in Toronto in the summer of 1959. My father had recently moved from his sister and brother-in-law's house in Eastern Ontario to be a boarder at Judith's sister's house in Toronto. My mother was struck by my father's sexual restraint toward her, interpreting this as a sign of respect rather than a differently oriented libido. My mother did not want to be a fading wallflower and jumped at the chance of marriage. She quickly prepared herself, getting her own small apartment in Toronto and leaving behind the family farm in Belleville.

My father had engaged in ongoing sexual escapades with young men during his teens, acting out the earlier sexual abuse he had suffered from older relatives. Sexual boundaries with some of those relatives were still a little blurry. Just before he met my mom, a woman Dad felt he loved had jilted him to take up with his older brother. Dad wanted the normality he thought marriage could bring, but he wanted that normality more as a cover than a sustaining reality. Were such a thing possible in the 1960s, he never would have wanted to marry another man. Instead, he wanted a subservient wife to cook, clean, and dote on his every need and demand, while she discreetly looked the other way during his frequent sexual dalliances with other men. The miserable truth of the matter is Dad had no way of knowing how to love and support a woman and probably never intended to do so.

My parents both came to the marriage with some secrets that would soon render their hastily arranged union unworkable. It was on their shoestring honeymoon in the country, traveling in an old car and staying at motels along the way, that my father discovered the needle my mother used to inject insulin into her thigh every morning to control her juvenile diabetes. He was horrified by the bizarre insulin reactions that developed periodically when she was under stress and was insulted that she had not told him about her medical condition.

My mother would have to wait a while longer for full revelation of my father's secrets but had a startling preview on their wedding night under the bed covers when she discovered him wearing her skimpy negligee and one of her bras with two full-sized grapefruits stuffed in their cups. At first, she hoped this was just some ridiculous prank, but she soon began to have some unsettling feelings of doubt about this early episode in their marriage. Could there be more my father had not told her?

The early weeks and months of marriage present a steep and challenging learning curve for any young couple, even when they are open and honest with each other. Distrust and mutual dishonesty, unfortunately, were the hallmarks of my parents' marriage right from the very beginning. In fact, my very conception was itself the fruit of deception.

One year into the marriage, Dad surreptitiously scrounged among Mom's toiletries in her upper dresser drawer and poked two holes in her contraceptive diaphragm with a needle. They had talked about having children, but my mother wanted to wait. I suppose the reason Dad was so eager to conceive was to prove to his family that he was normal. It did not take long before conception occurred in the spring of 1962, though my mother was almost five months pregnant before she realized what was up. After seeing her physician about how sick and dizzy she was feeling, she was sent immediately for further testing to a gynecologist who discovered her special surprise bundle. She did not feel ready for children and was furious when she found the holes in the diaphragm she always had kept hidden away. This ontogeny by stealth only served to drive my parents further apart.

One night while Mom was pregnant and resting in the bed next to Dad, she saw demons in the room, prancing around the bed and then escaping through an open window. This frightened her, but she did nothing about it; she was so overwhelmed with fear and dread. Dad thought she was just having another diabetic reaction and gave no attention to the matter. Later, she came to believe these spirits were linked to Dad's many sexual liaisons with men. What really disturbed me when I heard about this was that I had had very vivid dreams as a young child where I too saw demons dancing around my parents' bed.

At North Western General Hospital in Toronto, Mom was expecting twins. She had needed hospitalization and a lot of bed rest. My twin brother and I were not expected to live; we were breech and coming prematurely, and my mother's health was severely jeopardized by her diabetes. During her labor, Mom asked that God would take the lives of her children if we were not going to live for Him. Though this was a mother's honorable request, could she really affect my free choice and make it dependent on her prayer? Surely no one can be a programmed robot while having a true relationship with God. No one could set that up for me—not even my mother.

I was born in December 1962, just after midnight. My twin brother, Thomas, was born five minutes later—something I think he has vaguely resented ever since. Once issued out into the world, we were separated not just from the warm, dark womb but also from each other for the first time. I think real sadness and anger entered both of us at that point. We wanted to be in contact with each other in some way and be put back together. The incubators enclosed us, separating us in a sterile world of lights, doctors, and nurses. We were attended to for regular feedings and diaper changes without all the needed closeness that is now recommended for infants. Soon enough, Dad would establish his exasperating habit of avoiding nearly every milestone in his children's lives, but he was there to sign the birth certificates, and I was duly registered as Cynthia Dawn.

While my parents rented a tiny apartment in the back of a house in Toronto for the first few months of our lives, we soon moved into a three-level green and white duplex. My parents rented out the upper-floor bedrooms and bathroom of this house to boarders. The kitchen and living and dining areas were on the main floor. My parents, my brother, and I slept in the basement, which had a separate laundry room at the back behind a frosted, white-paned French door where there was a small window supplying the only natural light to the entire lower level. We lived next to a large and open park that had mature maple trees that offered shade during the hot summers. Sometimes we were taken out in a large red metal carriage that sprang and rocked over each bump in the sidewalk as we were pushed along. The beautiful trees would fly by overhead like green sailboats on an upside-down ocean of blue and white sky.

For the first three months, a nursemaid took care of us at night while Mommy slept, re-stoking her depleted energy to attend to us during the day. Mother was a petite, thin, and very ill woman. She had pale, white, Irish skin with striking, black, wavy hair that cascaded well below her shoulders. When the brilliant sun gleamed on her long hair, it took on an auburn tinge, highlighting the black coloring. Her deep, dark blue eyes were framed by almond-shaped, black-rimmed glasses that made her big eyes seem smaller than they actually were.

Mother was often fretful and overwhelmed as she struggled all alone with the unpredictable effects of her Type I diabetes. Her condition could set off mood swings and low-energy troughs at any time. Sometimes insulin reactions caused her to become overheated, incomprehensible, confused, and even to lose consciousness. She was very weak, and any stress could send her blood sugar too high or too low. To cope, she often put us down for afternoon naps that could last for hours at a time. The benefit of all of this was that she kept a strict routine of feeding, diaper changes, naps, and bedtime when Thomas and I were placed in our separate, high-edged cribs and covered with baby blankets. The downside was that Mother often would not come at night when one or both of us cried, as she believed that would spoil a child. I was not comforted, and this lack of attention laid the foundation for my later childhood, when I came to feel as if I were a burden. Dad was not available to assist much in our care because he was out working or spending time with friends, leaving my mother particularly overwhelmed with twins. During thunderstorms, this miserable loneliness and terror would creep into my soul as I longed to feel snugly secure. I experienced the desolation of not being wanted and not being worth the trouble of care.

These hours alone were mentally and emotionally agonizing. As we grew, Thomas and I would climb into each other's cribs to hold and comfort each other. But then Mom would come and put us back in our separate cribs again. The only time we were held was when we were being fed. Yet as soon as we could hold the bottles ourselves, we were left to gulp back our own formula without benefit of human contact. Thomas and I sat in chrome high chairs with vinyl cushions well away from the kitchen table until we had learned to eat properly with implements. This was demeaning and again fueled my feelings of not belonging and being unworthy of even the simplest human companionship.

Cutting me off from the world even a little more, I developed a stutter as I learned to speak. Mom admonished me over and over to be quiet and not to talk, while Dad was more inclined to correct my every mistake. Thomas and I were expected to do what we were told and were not allowed to express our feelings or thoughts openly. Small wonder in such a repressive household that a stutter would develop! I would suffer with this until the age of three when I began six years of speech therapy to overcome the embarrassing habit.

According to Mom, I cried most often because of bellyaches. I was often thirsty since the formula was the only liquid we got for the first year and a half. A woman at the church noticed that our scalps were covered in scaly, white flakes and realized that Thomas and I were not getting enough fluid. She told Mom that we were dehydrated and that she should give us water and juice to drink along with the formula.

When I was nearly three years old, Dad found out that Mom had given me a bottle with warm milk in it while he was out. I had just been potty-trained, finished wearing diapers, and was feeling quite grown up about these accomplishments. Having my milk heated could be seen as a step backward in my progress, the same sort of lapse that adults engage in when they partake of "comfort food." Asked to explain why she had given in like this, Mom said, "Cynthia was begging for a bottle, and she wouldn't leave me alone until I gave it to her."

My insides caved in as I felt that I had done something wrong and was now found out. My father came over and lifted me onto the kitchen table. "I'll show you what you have to wear if you don't stop acting like a baby," he said. In no time, he was fitting a cloth diaper around me and pinning it up while I shook nervously and cried.

Later that evening, while Dad was out at work, Mom came by and plunked a pacifier dipped in honey into my mouth as I lay pouting and crying in my crib. I was warned not to mention this consolation to Dad because it would upset him. Possibly, Mom wanted to rid herself of the guilt she felt for not nurturing me enough and was defiantly sneaking another form of solace to me—here, have this crumb, but don't tell your father. It was meant to soothe me, but I sensed her rushed and unsteady hand as she complained about my behavior. I resolved not to ask her to soothe me again for a while.

I had one stuffed animal, a pink cat that I slept with every night. Its coat had become quite worn, and it was probably in danger of splitting and losing some of its stuffing. One night, Mom came in and took it away. Though I cried to have it returned, she wouldn't budge. To compensate for this loss, I remember pulling feathers out of my pillow and using them to stroke my face and hands, providing some comfort to help me fall asleep.

Mom didn't have access to a vehicle, and she undoubtedly felt frustrated and trapped with the care of us as Dad was hardly ever at home in the evenings. When he was around, and as often as not, she received cutting remarks from him rather than encouraging words that would have affirmed her as a woman, wife, and mother. She often struggled with exhaustion by the end of the day and began putting her own needs and wants ahead of ours.

One evening, I fell down the basement stairs, hurting my legs and knocking the wind out of me, which was a very frightening sensation. In a breathless sort of panic, I cried in gasping bursts and was incredulous that my parents remained seated on the edge of their bed, waiting for me to pull myself up off the floor and go to them. The worst was over by the time I made my way over to their side, hoping at least to be held. But all they were dispensing that day were the quickest of hugs. This begrudging minimum of a sop didn't do a blessed thing to soothe my wounded heart.

Tellingly, one of the few consolations or satisfactions I distinctly recall from infancy was the feel and sound of the fasteners on our red and blue pants being done up one snap at a time. This was comforting to me as it meant I was now clean and dutifully dressed and I could go somewhere upstairs and wouldn't need my parents for a while.

Men and women boarders lived upstairs in our house for most of the five years we were there. They ate at different times than we did, which meant that we were not allowed to come up to the kitchen when we wanted to, not even to play. I hardly saw some of these cohabitants as they were often out. The only boarder we really came to know was Dennis, an old school friend of Dad's who lived with us for about five years.

My mother ran loads of laundry through an old, noisy, white wringer washer. Much of her time was spent taking care of the house, doing chores, and preparing meals. She was not one to play with us, as the simplest household duties overwhelmed her. Hearing nursery rhymes or lullabies, playing games, being rocked—these were all foreign to us. Nor did she read many stories to us.

Reading materials, coloring books, toys, and outings were scarce during my childhood. Any sort of physical or emotional nurturing was a rare delight in these early years. Whenever I saw Play-Doh or crayons at other kids' houses, I would gravitate to them for their texture, scent, and color, indulging myself in the whole experience of pounding, kneading, shaping, and coloring whatever I could get my hands on.

Because of his frequent absence, I always would associate a strange, mysterious wonder with my father. Daddy seemed to bring more adventure and curiosity into my life than my mother did. When he came home, he sometimes brought extra-large chocolate bars and gave us a few squares before bedtime. On some weekends after supper, he enjoyed pulling out a bag of cheesy snacks for us to munch on. He would have us sit quietly at the kitchen table while he doled out portions to Thomas and me.

Sometimes in the early mornings, I would enjoy those special times when Dad happened to be around. We lived quite poorly, even though Dad was working a lot, but some mornings there would be fried bacon and eggs; toast with real, creamy butter; and orange juice to drink. The CFRB (1010 A.M.) radio morning show provided a background chatter of voice and song; the sound of the newsreaders and the singers seemed to come out of nowhere, almost like birds flying from branch to branch in the surrounding atmosphere. My father was the figure who brought fun and otherwise forbidden nourishment into my life. Of course, I desired his close presence most of all, but that commodity was in such short supply, I settled instead for the food he brought.

Mom was similarly starved for Dad's affection and attention. Though I sometimes heard my parents talking in the kitchen, I don't ever remember them hugging or kissing or expressing any other gestures of affection. There were other things I could not understand as well. Why didn't Dad come home every night? I learned the answer a few years later.

It was hard for a farm boy to get a foothold in the big city, and at this time Dad was working four jobs. His main income derived from a paint company where he worked on the factory floor before moving on to office work. On the weekends, he mowed their lawns, having learned that taking on extra work often opened up more opportunities for advancement within a company. A number of years later, Dad told the story of how a man fell into a cylinder of paint and died, and Dad shuddered to think that could have been him. Dad also waited on tables at a restaurant and served as a janitor and a young people's leader at the little United Pentecostal church we attended. Dad also enrolled in a course in cost accounting, an evening class for which he would cram in the early-morning hours before going to work. With his energy and focus so diffracted by his many jobs and extracurricular nightlife, he never got through the first level. I just remember the dark, expensively bound business books that were neatly arrayed on the shelf like intellectual trophies.

Dad played an alto saxophone during his spare moments at home, on weekends usually. I loved hearing him play, even if it only lasted a few moments. I was not allowed to touch his sax or even be in the same room with him while he played. He thought I might break the hinged brass covers that went up and down over the holes as he played the notes. Some of the gospel songs had a jazzy, blue melancholy to them that I've always enjoyed. Even as a kid, such sadness—without reprieve or antidote—seemed a legitimate expression of my own emotions for which I longed someone to hear and answer. The saxophone has always represented a type of masculine beauty for me—the kind you not only hear but feel as it resonates all around and through you. It has always reminded me of my father's voice.

Disobedience was dealt with strictly. Mom would give us spankings each week when we didn't do things exactly as we were told. Her frustration and loss of support from Daddy left her feeling swamped. She had two thin sticks and two narrow belts, and sometimes she used the electrical cord from the fryer in the kitchen. Dad first introduced Thomas and me to the narrow sticks and straps when we were six or seven. They were there to threaten us and guide us toward good behavior through fear. His enthusiastic descriptions of the different kinds of whips and leather straps and rods available unsettled me. He further described how some whips had metal bits on the ends that could cut into skin. Because it was my mother who used them regularly on our bare back sides, I couldn't figure out why he'd brought them into our home.

Though she carried out the physical discipline in our household, Mom didn't enjoy beating us. But this was all she knew from her own childhood. I don't remember Dad ever hitting us. Indeed, he had vowed he wouldn't do that because of his own experience growing up with an abusive and alcoholic father. I deduced that the physical discipline he received must have been horrendous. On one level, Mom was very much in charge while we were growing up, as Dad so often was not at home. But on another level, I saw that he set the agenda. Like us, Mom was at my father's beck and call, submitting to him out of fear and carrying out his commands about everything from nutrition to discipline.

Away from both parents, Thomas and I would hide under the pantry porch at the back of the house whenever we wanted to pretend we were somewhere else. We also liked it when Mom filled the plastic wading pool with warm water from the green hose that snaked across the back lawn. We would take our few toys and dolls and place them in the water and watch them slosh about as we splashed in the hot sunshine. During the winter months, Thomas and I had green snowsuits with furry, white-trimmed hoods that we wore on the coldest days. We sometimes were able to go across the street to Monarch Park, where the snow looked blissfully pleasant and clean, like a white blanket. I remember each step making a crunching sound underfoot and my legs quickly tiring from the giant-sized steps I had to take to lift each foot out of the deep snow. We liked riding our sled down the hilly parts. A few years later, we walked deep into the park where there was a bridge underpass, even though we were told to never go there alone because this was a place where dangerous men hung out. A sense of impending danger always alerted me when I came near that spot.

Thomas and I learned to skate with a neighbor friend who was patient enough to watch us fall and get up again while we took our chances on a small rink in the park across the road. I couldn't get over the novelty of being told how well I had done when all I remembered was falling a lot.

When Thomas and I turned three, Dad's mom helped make two special birthday cakes—one pink and the other blue. It was already dark outside and the lights were turned out in the kitchen. We were told to sit down to have our pictures taken in the flickering glow of the candle-lit cakes. We each received one of Gran's hand-knitted sweaters, which we wore with pride. Birthdays were rarely celebrated with much fuss through the years, so it is my third birthday that I remember best. Dad was not there. It was as if Mom and Grandma were waiting for him to come home and then, realizing that it was late and Thomas and I needed to go to bed soon, they decided to go ahead without him, the camera flashing away and capturing our under-attended celebration.

Thomas and I were a part of twin studies in the sixties at the University of Toronto. Of all these sessions, I recall very little except the mirrors that lined an otherwise bare wall in a room with cold lighting. And there were different observation rooms. The session I remember best was the last one. As Thomas waited, I got to choose a doll that day from a wooden corner cabinet with illuminated glass shelves. The plastic dolls were warm to the touch and smelled of glue. Their clothing was simple with uncut loose threads. I couldn't decide between two dolls that I really liked, first choosing one, then the other, really wanting to take them both. When I came home, I immediately ran to the basement and sat on my white crib mattress next to my baby blanket. Alone down there while Thomas helped Mom make a meal upstairs, I tore off the doll's clothes and broke its small legs and threw them across the room toward the bottom of the basement stairs, an area I associated with danger and fear. This was impulsive behavior that disturbed me even as I did it. Why was I so angry? Had I ripped off the doll's legs so she couldn't get away either? So she would be just as stuck as I was?

T W O

Deep Longing

O ne very early morning, when I was three, I awoke earlier than usual in a state of emotional excitement. For some reason, I wanted to be made to feel particularly favored. I wanted to be taken up and embraced for a long time by Dad. I stood in my pajamas on the quilted comforter on my parents' double bed waiting in expectancy, watching as he set the silver metal cuff links into his white iron-pressed shirtsleeves and adjusted his tie in front of the dresser mirror. It was amazing to me how the tie could be a very long piece of dark, narrow cloth one moment and then become this neat two-layered stripe with a nifty knot that fitted into the collar.

Daddy abruptly turned around and said in a rushed voice, "I have to go to work." He did not meet my great need and expectation to be held that day. I was so looking forward to being hugged and kissed. He said he didn't have time, not realizing how much he had just crushed me on the inside. This had not been my first rejection, but that day I changed. I never approached him the same way again. Instinctively sensing that he would never be there for me in the way that I needed him to be, I turned away from him and began to search for a father substitute to supply attention and tenderness. I unconsciously hunted for a familiar male image to repair the many injuries to my psyche. That image was often found in the face of a male in authority. I did not realize at the time how deep my longings were for my father. Without a secure attachment to Dad, I could not similarly connect to any other male in my life or even relate to God the Father. My aloofness only would be removed by exposing my spirit and soul to God's genuine love and touch many years later.

I remember going to church and wanting desperately to be held one particular Sunday. I watched the parishioners going into the small sanctuary with rows of pews on both sides separated by a main aisle that led to the raised platform where the pastor spoke at a podium. On a good Sunday, attendance could be over a hundred people. I would be allowed to sit quietly with Mom during the musical praise portion and then I would be ushered quickly to the darkened nursery area at the back. After the service, I again would be able to be stand next to my mother. Dad was away downstairs, teaching a Sunday school class.

As I stood in the hallway next to the pastor this day, I waited for him to notice me. The pastor had a daughter my age who I knew from Sunday school, so it would not have been that unusual for him to pick up children and hold them. The pastor wore a dark suit and white shirt and his height was similar to Dad's. His dark blond hair was neatly combed back off his high smooth forehead, and his skin was a healthy, light, golden color with inset blue eyes.

His face looked different up close than from a distance. I preferred looking at him from a distance.

As I approached him, I bravely asked if I could have a hug. He caught me just as I jumped up into his arms. I was able to get a big squeeze as I wrapped my little legs halfway around him tightly, rubbing my groin area against his waist. I felt vulnerable and embarrassed for needing this, and for some reason getting an embrace from him was not as satisfying as I first had trusted it would be. My humiliated mother marched over and hissed that I was not to do that ever again. I felt ashamed for my scattered feelings. I just wanted Daddy, but he was not there.

Over Christmas that December, I had to have surgery for a blocked tear duct, a symbolically significant condition that didn't allow me to cry properly. I don't remember how long I was at the hospital, but I remember being left alone quite a bit and wondering where my parents were. My mother was in the hospital due to a difficult pregnancy, though nobody had bothered to tell me, and my father was probably relieved not to have to watch over me. Nurses put a gown on me with long wooden sticks in the sleeves so I wouldn't be able to bend my elbows to scratch off my eye patch. My eye was itchy all the time. To take my mind off things, I played with all of the toys in a small playroom that was lavishly decorated with garlands and wreaths. All alone, I reveled in this enchanting Christmas atmosphere, so much richer than anything we ever had at home.

After what seemed a week or so, I came home with a patch on one eye. I don't remember any homecoming celebration, just disappointment in coming home to our drab and stark house. It was a few days after Christmas when I returned, and there was a small doll with white shoes, a brown and white puppy pull toy, and a red 3-D View Master left for me under the obligatory and barely decorated tree. None of these items had even been wrapped. I felt a lot of disappointment that I had missed Christmas with Daddy and Thomas, but there seemed to be no choice in the matter. Though it was extravagantly celebrated in other households, Christmas was not a special family-centered time of year for us, even though we were ostensibly Christian. This only added to the sensory deprivation I already felt in so many areas of my life. And if we weren't close in ways that families should be, I was already starting to detect that we were way too intimately connected in ways that families never should be.

My parents had taken movies of Thomas and me naked after our bath as we climbed over each other. Though I didn't have any memory at the time of pictures being taken, there were two reels of film that would resurface later in my life, causing much embarrassment. In these films, my mother placed Thomas and me on her feet so that we straddled her ankles for bumpy rides. At other times, Dad and Mom took Thomas and me to bed with them. It was hard to remember this stuff, to know if we dreamed it or it actually happened, but Thomas and I sometimes would share our secrets about Dad and Mom.

During one of our last baths together, Thomas asked about the dreams he had had about Mommy and Daddy. "Dawn, do you remember sucking on Mom's and Dad's dooties?" "Dooties" was our twin talk for "breasts." I quietly shared with him that I did and that I also had had these horrible nightmares of being placed all over Mommy's and Daddy's naked bodies. In the dreams, Thomas recalled Daddy placing his big "monkey" on his buttocks. He asked,

"Have you had those kinds of dreams?" I quietly leaned against him whispering, "No, Daddy did not do that to me in the dreams." We were too afraid to speak about any of this to adults.

At night, I began having different paralyzing nightmares that lasted seven years. These were strange, mystifying dreams that had fearful passages and sexual overtones. In these nightmares, I recall my total inability to control my surroundings. There was this sense of flying through the air, as if raised up by hands on my sides while suspended above my parents. As the terrible dreams proceeded, I was placed on different parts of my parents' naked legs and torsos. There were some frustrating sexual feelings awakened in these episodes, but I had no words for them. Afraid of the nightmares and not understanding why I was having such thoughts about Mommy and Daddy who could do no wrong, I had an incriminating sense that I was a bad girl.

The terror of these nightmares was repeated over and over again. It was as if some cruel machine in my head went on rewind and replay every night. I was too ashamed to talk about them with anyone, believing I was wholly responsible for such fevered nocturnal imaginings. I couldn't discern yet that these nightmares of shattered innocence and trust had grown out of what I actually had seen and experienced.

While pregnant with our younger brother, Mom had gone away to the hospital for eight months, off and on, to have her toxemia monitored. This was never explained to me, nor do I remember visiting her. Dad hated hospitals, so I gather he didn't want to take us to see her. Women from the church and Grandma came over to help out. Dennis, the boarder, took care of Thomas and me when he was home. Already, there was this unusual closeness between

Dad and Dennis. Dennis would often talk with Dad, and I couldn't help noticing that they seemed a lot closer than Dad and Mom and that Dad respected him more and treated him better. Dad frequently berated Mom in front of us and his friends, throwing off snide comments like, "Judith can't even cook, and look how fat her behind is." He even said that when Mom only weighed about 125 pounds.

Dennis taught Thomas and me our numbers and the alphabet as we sat on the floor in the upstairs' front room of his apartment. He showed us how to print our names and write out simple words. Though we often forgot some of his lessons, he always was kind and friendly toward us. I thought of him as a family member, more like an older brother than a boarder. He had a television set by the window that we sometimes were allowed to watch. One program that we particularly enjoyed was the *Flintstones*. We identified like crazy with Pebbles and Bam-Bam.

In the same way that I was seeking out substitute father figures, other women started emerging in my life, providing me with unconditional love and acceptance. These women were often mothers themselves who might simply step next to me, with a hand on the shoulder that let me know someone cared. One particular older woman, who had never married and who lived with her sister in a beautiful old duplex, was generous to me when I was a very young girl. She was a rather mature woman, in her sixties, with pin-curled white hair netted back off her plain face. She was highly regarded as a godly woman in our church who often watched after children, cooked meals, and did light cleaning to help out young families. Her name was Grace, but I called her Aunt Grace.

One Sunday morning after church, she asked my parents if I could stay at her house on a Saturday night, once in a while, to help lighten the load for Mom who was then going through her difficult pregnancy. My parents had no problem letting Aunt Grace take care of me, as she was trustworthy and kind. Thomas was a little jealous that I got to go over first, but he would get his turn later, and we would both return many times.

The first night I stayed over, we ate supper together and then talked for a while in her sitting room. As bedtime approached, she showed me where the washroom was so I could get changed, brush my teeth, and ready myself for bed. It was novel to me that there was not the usual nudity I was accustomed to at home with my parents. When I came out of the washroom, she let me know where I could put my few belongings. I had wondered when she was going to put the hard, rubber curlers in my hair, but she told me to not worry as she planned on using a curling iron in the morning. She too had changed into her flannelette nightgown, housecoat, and slippers. When I was ready, she pulled out a smaller rolling daybed that adjoined hers. She placed crisp sheets on each of the mattresses, gently rubbing out the wrinkles. Then I helped her with the top sheets and blankets.

As she readied the room for the night, I climbed into my bed and pulled the covers up to my face. "Now I'm going to turn out the lights," she announced. "Good night." Then, she got into her bed and that was it. I felt so incredibly relieved. "Good night," was all there was. The lights went out. Nothing else happened. She was quiet, and I could fall asleep in peace. I lay there in the darkness for quite a while, luxuriating in this sense of wholesome security that Aunt Grace provided.

Her breakfasts were superb. She would have me come to the small kitchen to sit down at a table for two while she asked me what I wanted to eat—cold cereal in the summer, hot oatmeal in the winter, a bran muffin with butter, or eggs boiled or scrambled with toast. While I waited, I often would look outside the narrow kitchen window and watch the various birds coming to the feeder outside the birdhouse. Birds approached the sill, singing and chirping, looking out for bugs and worms, and finding seed inside the feeder. I often would be so enthralled with this display, I would forget all about breakfast until she served it to me. Her willingness to serve a child made me feel somehow that I belonged on earth. Hers seemed the type of love that might be shown by Christ Himself.

Aunt Grace spoke about how things were and not about how they appeared. She knew that Dad was not always home a lot and why. There had been a questionable incident around this time, involving Dad and a pastor at a campground. They were sharing the same bed and Dad had awakened, rolled over, and put his arm around the pastor and touched his groin area. Dad said that in his unconscious state, he thought the pastor was Mom. This caused a humiliating uproar among the church members, and many found out about it. The pastor ended up leaving the church, and Dad no longer attended much after that.

Aunt Grace also knew about Dad's other sexual activities involving his friend Dennis, who had been living with us for almost as long as I could remember. I could not understand all of what she said or how she knew so much, but I instinctively trusted her when she said, "Cynthia, I know about the people who live in your house and that your father is not always home. This is hard for you. Your dad is not living as he should. I want you to know that God loves you and I am praying for you to be strong."

Sometimes I felt uncomfortable that she knew so much about my family. But her words rang true to me, so I kept listening to her. She spoke about the things that no one in our house was allowed to discuss. She never was judgmental or angry with my father. As I got older, she sometimes would say to me in a serious tone, "Your daddy should be going to church. He is doing things he ought not to be doing. They are wrong. He is out with men rather than at home with his family."

It was strange hearing her talk about my father and mother the way she did. Aunt Grace spoke to me like I was a real person who one day would have to choose what kind of life I was going to live. She reminded me that I had to honor and obey my parents and leave them with God. This was challenging for me as I was already discerning the ways in which our family was not like others. I would be morally torn for years between compliantly obeying my father even if he asked me to do something wrong, and choosing not to obey him by doing what was right. Thomas and I continued our visits to Aunt Grace until we were twelve and moved away from the neighborhood.

When Mom came home in late February of 1966, there was a baby brother, Scott, who I absolutely adored and who adored me in return. He was warm, soft, cuddly, and happy, and his blue eyes sparkled with mischievous laughter. I would touch his soft hands and face every opportunity I had, lavishing the kind of affection on him that I had never known. We played constantly, and as we got older, I took him for carriage rides, back and forth along the sidewalk.

Finally, we moved upstairs in the house, and Dennis took a room at the end of the hall next to our bedroom. My father got bunk beds for Thomas and me, while baby Scott was kept in his crib in our room by the door. I was excited to try out the top level and see what it was like to fall out, but Dad quickly nixed that idea by tightly nailing in the outside railings. My parents shared the front room where Dennis had been, though many nights Dad did not come home.

Thomas and I started junior kindergarten at Earl Haig Public School in the fall. I don't recollect much of JK, but I do of kindergarten. Thomas and I played together a lot in the kitchen and block areas. I also liked doing the animal puzzles and painting on the easels. My artistic slant did not materialize that early. I just drew pictures of houses, birds, grass, and flowers over and over. Somehow, I thought that was what was expected, so I did it. When the teacher wanted me to do something unique, I would draw pictures of small sailboats and blue waves of water, thinking of Jesus on the water. There was a boy in the kindergarten class who I liked a little because he looked so cute. I kept this to myself, as I felt innately ashamed of these types of feelings. Also, I'd sometimes seen teachers ridicule children who expressed their early childhood crushes.

When I was five, we moved to a house near the Danforth and Woodbine area in Toronto, a house where we didn't have to take in boarders. One summer weekend, wielding a soapy sponge to help Dad clean the car, I asked why Dennis was no longer living with us. The car radio was blaring as he flatly answered, "You're not going to see Dennis again."

"Why not?" I asked, alarmed by the finality of it all.

Without looking at me, Dad said, "He's no longer my friend." And that was that. I missed Dennis, but what I didn't realize then was that there would be a whole series of relationships that my father would become entangled in and then abruptly curtail. It was the lack of an explanation that bothered me, since I always had had Dennis in my life from as far back as I could remember.

While Dad and Mom were out, Larry started coming by to visit and babysit my brothers and me. He was another friend of Dad's. I didn't particularly like him. He'd get angry with me easily for not doing what he said. During a hide-and-seek game, Larry became so exasperated with me that he locked me in the bedroom closet and walked away. Unfortunately, my baby finger got wedged in the door and was bleeding profusely by the time he finally let me out.

"You hurt me! You hurt me!" I screamed as he scampered about with a tissue, asking me to hold it on my finger while he went looking for bandages. When my parents came home, Mom wrapped my finger with a number of Band-Aids, and Dad was so furious, he vowed Larry would never come around again—and he didn't.

We already had started attending Gled Hill Public School for grades one through six. At this time, teachers started calling me by my middle name, Dawn, instead of my first, Cynthia. This was an adjustment at first, and I felt that I somehow took on a new beginning as a person. Mom told me the reason for the name change was because Thomas had been calling me "Cyn" for short, and my parents thought this homonym for "sin" gave a wrong connotation to my name. Another huge change was that Thomas and I were assigned different classrooms and would be until grades five and six, so we could learn to work more independently.

I had no voice in the family and had depended heavily on Thomas to speak up for me due to my problem with stuttering. Also, Thomas was the only one who fully understood our "twin" language, those special words and phrases that had meaning only for us. Wrenching as the separation was, I could see its necessity. I started to develop in ways I wouldn't have if Thomas had still been by my side. Both of us benefited from the separation, though it seemed awfully cruel at the time. We took turns doing better at certain subjects and became quite competitive. There were times I got to peek into his classroom, and it always seemed strange to see him leading a separate existence.

One day in grade one, I had an impulse to carefully lift my dress. Making sure the teacher wasn't looking, I pulled aside my underwear, uncovering my private area as I spread my little legs. I wanted to know how the boys and girls would react. Would they even notice? Would this make some of my strange nightmares end? The children reacted with noisy shock and disbelief. As soon as the teacher found out, she called me to the coatroom for a spanking. I remember leaning over her lap as she smacked me on the behind once. It seemed a light punishment compared to what I got at home. I then was instructed quietly to never do that again.

The very next moment, I defiantly did the very same thing again, and some students tattled on me. To make it more embarrassing, this time I was verbally corrected in front of my classmates. Ashamed, I began to realize that the sort of sexual frankness to which I was exposed at home was not acceptable at school. I was taken for another spanking and assigned to write out the alphabet one hundred times during an after-school detention. The teacher phoned Mom, who gave me another spanking when I got home, telling me to never do that again. I was confused because I was being disciplined for acting out an aspect of what I saw all the time at home. Both parents routinely walked around nude in front of us. Dad, in particular, had precious little sense of boundaries and decency around us. What was the difference between that sort of behavior and my showing myself to other children?

We started swimming lessons at an inside pool at Monarch Park School that summer. These were most enjoyable for me, as I always loved the freedom of the water about me and quickly progressed to higher levels of accomplishment as a swimmer. In the change rooms, I came up against some unexpected taunting from some girls when I tried to get dressed with a towel wrapped around me. One girl came over and tugged at it while mocking me. Later that summer, some girls from another grade one class met me at the swings and asked if I was the girl who'd shown off her privates in class. I became embarrassed and denied I was the girl. I was receiving mixed signals to say the least. Sometimes it was wrong to expose myself and sometimes it was wrong to keep myself covered up. My home life was no help at all in understanding these mysteries.

A couple of years after this, I happened upon a Bible passage that told parents not to show their nakedness to their children. I remember reading Leviticus 18:6-8 to Mom and Dad in their bedroom, feeling very awkward but assured that somehow this scripture spoke what I was too afraid to say by myself. This made some difference. They began to cover up more often, though Dad did not do it that consistently. Even during my teen years, he occasionally paraded around in his underwear.

Even when Dad took me out to the park on a little outing, his attentions were otherwise engaged. One time, when I was still in grade one, he took me to Woodbine Beach, where there were swings, slides, and a teeter-totter in the playground area. I was nervous about him pushing me on a swing, but I hesitantly got on anyway. As he distractedly pushed, I sensed his absence. As usual, I was not his primary concern. He was far more interested in the other men passing by and made vulgar comments about their physiques, especially their back ends.

While we were out grocery shopping with my father, he would snatch produce off stacked displays of fruit and hand some to us. He would also scrounge for snack foods out of once-sealed bags that had been partially split open. Were these acts like little white lies? Wasn't it still stealing if you took a small amount of something that did not belong to you? What was a child to learn from this? That stealing a little was all right?

Growing up, my father routinely took rhubarb and apples from neighboring orchards and farms. In the country, he probably could have gotten away with this sort of filching, but the rules were very different in city shops. One day, I was sent to the top of the street to get a few food items with my brother. While in the store, I did exactly what I'd seen my father do: I grabbed some popped popcorn from an open bag on the lower shelf. The manager of the store caught me. I was absolutely bewildered. I told the manager, "The bag was open so I grabbed some. My father does this."

It did not matter; I was advised to never frequent this grocery store again. So the next time I had to pick up a few groceries, I walked farther down Danforth Avenue to Becker's to get milk and bread. It was later I realized that not only was this a form of shop-lifting, but I could have been prosecuted.

Dad had high expectations for me academically. He tried to teach me a few things such as how to tell time, but I was so worried about not getting it right that I couldn't concentrate. I had trouble concentrating on lessons at school as well and would blank out if put on the spot. I felt stupid compared to my classmates, afraid of doing something wrong and being punished or ridiculed at school and then again at home. In grade one, I was placed in the weakest reading group. I got nervous whenever I was asked to read aloud or answer questions. Misplacing pieces of paper and notes, I often forgot to study beforehand for quizzes or tests. I was so confused and stressed that teachers thought I must be lying and disciplined me for not telling the truth.

Early one morning at school, some of the girls at my table unaccountably started shrieking that my eye was bleeding. I looked at the scissors in my right hand that I had been using to cut out some crafts, and realized that my head had somehow fallen onto the scissors, just a half inch from my eye. I had apparently blacked out and was now being rushed to the vice principal's office to be quickly escorted home to my worried mother. A cold, wet cloth was given to me to hold over my eye during the drive home, and then Mom took me to the hospital for stitches. Though I never had quite so dramatic a blackout as this one again, I continued to misplace items, have no recall of some lessons learned, and found myself unable to cope with the daily tension at school and at home.

When I was six, there was another round of surgery to open a blocked tear duct in my other eye. This time, I was much more independent, brushing my own teeth, bathing myself, and dressing myself. I conversed with the nurses a lot, especially the night after my surgery. The contents of my stomach did not stay down in response to the anesthesia. I recall the crisp white bed sheets being changed no less than four times. It took a lot of patience to put up with me that night. I enjoyed the extra attention no matter how I got it. I recall talking with a teenager one other evening when I felt very alone and being flattered that she would deign to talk to someone so much younger.

Mom came by for a short visit, but before long she was away again. My insides sank, as I could not bear the thought of another night away from home. Daddy, of course, didn't visit at all. I don't remember much in the way of a welcoming fanfare when I got home from this hospital stay either.

Family (Dys) Functions

S ometimes my parents, my brothers and I would go for trips
to Eastern Ontario. These trips often included a visit to the
Sandbanks, and my mother's parents' home or a visit to
my father's mother. Mommy often would drive us to her parents
alone, leaving Dad for time off with his joy-boys. Mother was often stressed out and exhausted, and this was just the kind of state
that could set off an insulin reaction, so Thomas and I knew to
pass her a chocolate bar from her purse if her driving started to
become erratic.

When Grandpa and Grandma retired, they moved to a doll-
house-sized trailer in a poorer area of Belleville. The side door led
into a small eat-in kitchen with windows on two sides to let in
light. To the left was a very small front sitting room with a La-Z-Boy
reclining chair. Grandpa and Grandma shared the front bedroom,
while Uncle Edward had the back bedroom. Sometimes we would
stay the night with my brothers and me sharing the couch that
opened into a bed.

My grandfather was an active farmer and gardener who loved his home-grown beans, carrots, potatoes, and corn. His tomatoes were particularly delicious. Grandpa would grind his own wheat kernels into coarse flour before making honey wheat and bran muffins for snacks. He used well water from a pail that sat on the kitchen counter. Sometimes I would go out and pump the water from the well. I found the water had a sullied taste to it, depending on the time of year.

What most enthralled me about my grandpa was when he would talk about the Bible and end times. He could go on for hours with a new rendition each visit, and I would sit, listening and imagining all the scenarios. It might seem strange for a six year old to be so engrossed in stories of the Apocalypse, but these accounts were suffused with a sense of justice and righteousness that was absent on those rare occasions when my father talked to me about the Bible. They also reinforced the idea that I needed to make good choices in my life. Sometimes I was afraid, but Grandfather would reassure me that I would be all right when all this came to pass. I loved listening to the audiotapes of a Christian brother who was a special speaker at camp meetings. I enjoyed my grandfather's prayers and hospitality, and whenever I asked questions, he would happily explain some more. He loved an audience, and I spent hours with him when I could.

My grandmother, on the other hand, had epilepsy with full-generalized seizures when she didn't take her medication. She was often quiet and unresponsive to what was going on, so Grandpa did most of the cooking and cleaning up. Sometimes she snapped at me when I got into things that I should not have. I came to understand, years later, why my mother never learned how to nurture children.

Here was the example before me. My grandmother was a Victorian Christian woman who wore long, dark-colored dresses and an ivory Lady Camille on a simple gold necklace around her neck. She often had a frown on her face and a no-nonsense strictness in her voice. But one good thing she knew was how to pray.

Great-Uncle Edward was a younger brother of Grandma, and he never married. He always wore thick black suspenders over white long-sleeved shirts with dark dress pants. He was a little slow because he was born with the umbilical cord wrapped around his neck, which cut off oxygen to his brain for a few minutes. I was curious as to why he lived with his sister and brother-in-law at such an age. Apparently, he had a lawn care business in Picton for a while and managed money well. Now, he was waiting to move into a nearby nursing home as Grandma could no longer take care of him. He was a gentle soul, and I'm sorry I avoided him as much as I did. Compared to Dad's family, however, Mom's upbringing had been idyllic.

My dad's mother was always part of our lives, but we only met his father a few times. Grandpa—who was Grandma's first cousin—died in his fifties of a heart attack, leaving Grandma blessedly alone. She had mainly raised her seven children by then. My dad was the second youngest. Grandma would sometimes come over to visit. She cooked a little walnut or chocolate fudge or baked thick peanut butter cookies for us kids. I was always amazed at her energy and enthusiasm. She enjoyed life even after living through two World Wars and the Great Depression. She spoke her mind easily and cannily, and when she didn't agree with something, she would let you know. We visited her at the farmhouse where Dad had grown up. I enjoyed the winding stairs that led to the top floor.

Grandma's home was cozy, warm, and cluttered with old black and white mezzotints from the turn of the century. I also liked the old dilapidated barn, where the cows and sheep were kept, and the chicken coop. Most of all, I liked the rabbits and other small animals that lived on the farm.

Because she could not go upstairs easily, she once made a bath for me in the kitchen in an old metal bathtub. She boiled kettles of water on the stove and poured them into this tub. I got to use white Dove soap, and it was such a special treat to have a bath this old-fashioned way. She was very kind to my brother and me. I think we exhausted her when we once stayed five days in a row when we were older.

I would enjoy walks up the main street of the town, past the old post office, the Woolworth's, the little movie theater, and the main library. I enjoyed looking at the trees that lined the streets in this neighborhood where even the humblest shacks had carefully tended gardens. Lilacs bloomed in spring in many people's yards, and through the summer we saw red and white geraniums, pansies, and impatiens. The smell of summer in the country was ravishing to this city-raised kid.

During World War II, my grandfather and some of Dad's older brothers went away to fight. Grandma had to take care of the children herself with precious little assistance from the church family. She had so little money that I don't know how she fed, clothed, and raised the younger children. My father and all of his brothers shared one small, unheated bedroom in the old farmhouse. He would wake up freezing cold with snow piled inside the window after a stormy winter's night. Dad learned to work all aspects of the farm, often getting up before dawn to feed the animals and clean their pens before heading off to the one-room schoolhouse. He had to work extra hard at school to make good marks and was very proud of himself when he finished grade thirteen. After all, only he and one other brother had made it through high school.

Dad did not see much of his father for the first five years of his life. In retrospect, that would be Dad's golden era. When his father came home in 1945, things changed a lot. If Dad were lucky then, he'd only be neglected. There were stories of being left outside the town's bar in an old, unheated farm truck for hours on end while his father went inside to drink, leaving his son cold, hungry, and scared as his father frittered away the afternoon and evening.

Much later, Dad told me that he was physically and sexually abused repeatedly. It happened so often, he was wounded beyond all natural repair. Grandfather would physically assault my grandmother and sexually abuse his daughter, Bea. The effects of Bea's epilepsy were worsened by the horrific stress she endured. Much later, Dad told me that he repeatedly heard Bea's screams in the barn where her father and some of Dad's older brothers took turns gang-raping her. According to my father, she suffered a stroke and had a lot of difficulties emotionally and physically because of her injuries, including paralysis on one side of her body. She was put on medications, suffered severe depression, and lived with her mother before dying in her early forties. These were shameful family secrets that were rarely mentioned openly, though their muffled aftereffects could flare up at the most unexpected times.

Thomas and I were outside sitting on the curb of the driveway one day, innocently imitating to each other how Aunt Bea's hand was always bent across at the first few knuckles of the fingers. Unknown to us, this was the legacy of her rape-induced stroke.

Suddenly, my father loomed over us, both of us squinting to make out his face as we looked up into the sun just behind his head. He told us in a stern voice that we were never to make fun of anyone with a disability, especially our Aunt Bea. We didn't understand the reason for his touchiness until much later, but Aunt Bea's afflictions obviously represented the very worst aspects of his past and the home he'd grown up in.

I enjoyed Dad's few happier recollections of childhood, but the sadder stories unnerved me and provided me a glimpse into why he lived his adult life in such precarious circumstances, taking risks and trying various ways to anesthetize the stark psychological pain that he so seldom shared with anyone. One can see why mercy and compassion are so needed in remembering my father. He had a harder life than I did in many respects and overcame much adversity. If only he had known love, acceptance, belonging, and healing! As a teenager, he needed glasses and couldn't read the blackboard at school. Dad said his classmates teased him for his near-sightedness, but I think there was something more behind the ridicule than that. Word had leaked that Dad and one of his male schoolmates were having a sexual relationship. He left home when he was fifteen after his father tried to run him over with the farm tractor, during one of Grandfather's tyrannical drunken rampages. Shaken and appalled that his own father had tried to kill him, Dad went to live with his older sister and her husband in Eastern Ontario before moving to Toronto and meeting my mother. By age twenty, he was married to my mom, and by age twenty-two, he had twins.

Grandma lived in an apartment before moving to a little flat in a small town and always made us feel at home even though she had her hands full with the care of my Aunt Bea. Despite her permanently deformed hand, Bea was a gifted weaver who created artistic designs with her hands, winning accolades and teaching others her techniques. I was amazed at her ability to use consistent tension as she wove decorative designs, using small, handheld frames. The weft was woven back and forth through the warp to make beautiful tablecloths and mats.

I know that occupational therapies such as basket weaving often serve as a sort of shorthand code for craziness that stand-up comics use in their routines. But that fact only magnifies for me the stark horror of Bea's plight as well as the poignancy of her recovery as far as she was able to take it. This was a good and talented woman—only a girl when she was all but destroyed by the men in her life who should have been watching out for her. Yet even after they did their very worst to her, in this one small corner of her life, Bea would not allow herself to be utterly extinguished. Insignificant and pitiful as her weaving might appear by worldly standards, I see a kind of victory here that can move me to tears. As one who suffered much less and still struggles daily to throw off the nihilistic effects of my upbringing, I take courage and hope from my aunt's unwitting example.

During my seventh summer, Dad helped us build a red wooden go-cart in which we could sit and propel ourselves with our feet up and down the sidewalk. Dad was pleased that he initiated this, as if to make up for previous years of neglect, but it was a little too late, as we were now too big to really enjoy this car. We went along with the project, as much for him as ourselves, knowing we wouldn't have to wait long before his attention drifted away to other things. Even when we borrowed a cottage from an elderly couple in the church, Dad was unable to stay around with his family for a complete week. Perhaps out of self-defense, we were learning to tune him out before he could do the same to us.

Dad set up Thomas and me to sell household cleaning products and greeting cards door-to-door after school and on weekends even though we were quite young. He wanted us to learn the value of a dollar, but we did not get to keep any of it. In the autumn, we were dropped off in a well-to-do neighborhood just off O'Connor Drive, next to Taylor Creek Park and far from home, and told to sell Regal products—Christmas cards and wrapping paper—door-to-door to make some extra money for a trip to Florida. There was no access to washrooms, and we did not have water bottles. Sometimes we had some snacks. We had no way of getting back home but to wait for Dad to come pick us up. So in addition to housework and homework, I found myself rapidly taking on far more responsibility than my friends had. It made me feel nervous inside and afraid that I could make a mistake, but it probably helped to prepare me for what lay ahead. Taking on these extra responsibilities made us less reliant on Mom with her dodgy health, which was about to take a dramatic turn for the worse. And Dad may have felt that he would not have to take on so much responsibility for us if we grew up fast. He could go where he wanted with his friends without worrying about us.

One day I was the first to come home from school. It was pouring rain and my clothes were soaked right through. I walked up the steps to the front porch door and found it locked. I started knocking loudly and could see my mother slouched against the wall as she sat by the telephone in the front hall. She didn't respond to my yells to open the door, and I realized that she must be having a major diabetic insulin reaction. Instead of checking the back door,

I cried out in shock, wondering what to do. A next-door neighbor came over, looked through the screen, and calmly took my hand and told me to come with her. She had children of her own and I trusted her. She took me to her place and had me take a very warm bath while she got help for my mom. By the time I had gotten out of the tub and dressed, my brothers were being taken care of by this dear neighbor, and we stayed with her until Mom revived.

That evening, Mom was very upset with us. She kept saying, "Why didn't you come to the back door? How could you? Now everyone is going to know about me." I didn't say much as I felt ashamed of what had happened. I was instructed if this happened again that I was to provide Mom with an emergency glass of orange juice and sugar.

That winter, we had our only birthday party with other children and school friends invited. My parents laid on hot dogs and ice cream and arranged for games of Pin the Tail on the Donkey and a candy hunt before we opened our presents. When it turned out that we did not receive much in the way of gifts, Dad decided that birthday parties were too much trouble and vowed we never would have another one. And we never did.

We decorated the Christmas tree and the living room that year with homemade decorations. We never had done this before and never would again. There were big gifts arranged under the tree and all three kids were excited. Dad had a good paying job, but we didn't fully understand that he was living a double life that was draining a lot of his income away. That summer, he had traveled to a gay hangout in Nassau with another man and dropped plenty of money there. At first glance, all we could see was that we never had had so many Christmas gifts before. Unknown to us, they were mostly used and badly battered toys. Maybe Dad was making another belated attempt to be more of a father to us, but again it was too little too late.

My sense of expectation turned to ashes when I unwrapped a broken doll and a used ironing board. My brothers' gifts were all used as well. Mom's only present was a sample of small bottles of different fragrances in a rectangular box. I felt hurt and worthless, both for her and myself. I ran upstairs, trying to be thankful for what I had just received. But I couldn't keep back the tears. We had worked so hard to make Christmas great that year, and yet all our efforts ended in this. I felt so sad for my twin brother who had made and put up all the decorations. He never again made a big deal of Christmas.

Most children love tradition and celebration. Reacting against our disappointment, my brothers and I started playing Christmas by ourselves, exchanging used pencils, erasers, and pennies as gifts to each other. I later realized Dad simply could not handle birthdays, holidays, or Christmases due to the unhappy memories they evoked of his childhood. So he either was not around on those days or would develop his own half-hearted substitutes, sometimes on Boxing Day.

That summer, Dad surprised us with bikes, though he didn't bother teaching us how to ride them. A nice East Indian man who lived next door took on that job, taking Thomas and me over to the schoolyard, where he taught us how to pedal and keep our balance. Once Thomas and I learned to ride, Dad would sometimes take us for bike rides through Taylor Creek Park, a well-known gay cruising area.

That same summer, Steve, who was only eighteen, became a fixture in our home, showing up at any time of day and walking through all parts of the place as if it were his own. Mom didn't seem to mind. A few times, I came upon Steve brushing Mom's hair off her face and styling it. Sometimes they'd go out shopping together. He'd cook meals in our kitchen if he felt a little peckish or stretch out on the couch for a nap. Steve also started playing card and board games on weekend nights with my brothers and me, even laying on a chips and dip spread. We thoroughly enjoyed the attention, as Dad never would sit still long enough to play games with us. Dad would grumble when he came home late from the office and found us still up with Steve, playing. I believe Dad was jealous of the closeness that developed between Steve and his children and may have worried about Steve hitting on the boys.

Steve's younger brother started coming over to the house for a few weekends as well, but that didn't last long. I never even got to know his name. We had just returned from strawberry picking, and I was out on the back patio washing the berries in a pail of water, when I heard loud talking in the kitchen between Dad and Mom. Something horrible had happened to one of Dad's friends. I came inside, sat down at the end of the kitchen table, and attentively listened. Dad's face was downcast, and he wouldn't look at me. Tears filled his eyes and he petulantly said, "I don't know why I have to go down and identify the body. How did the police even get my name?"

Apparently, Steve's younger brother had committed suicide by jumping off a high-rise building, and the police called Dad to come down and identify him. It was obvious that Dad felt responsible somehow and tried to console Steve. I wondered what was going on. I had overheard that Mom had found love notes from different boyfriends crushed up and thrown in the garbage. Apparently, she had told a few friends that Dad and some of these boyfriends were having sex in my brothers' and my bedroom when we weren't there. Could Dad have been fooling around with Steve and his brother at the same time? Was it possible that the brother left some kind of note identifying Dad and that was why the police wanted to see him?

Shortly after Steve's brother killed himself, another friend of Dad's came by to babysit us. Paul took us for a trip on the subway, and back at home we watched as he dipped strawberries in dark melted chocolate and perfectly placed the tantalizing treats on a cookie sheet that he set in the freezer. When Dad came home and discovered the freezer was full of dipped strawberries, he flew into a rage. He had planned to give Paul a piece of his mind. And I guess he did, because a week or so later Paul too was dead. He killed himself in the very same way as Steve's brother. I was devastated and would eventually learn to hold back and not get to know Dad's male lovers. Dad typically treated relationships like they were to be used for a time and then disposed of once they turned sour for whatever reason. It was almost like he fired them when they no longer were of use to him.

I was amazed that these lovers didn't run into each other as they popped in and out of our house, always calling exclusively at the back door. Gary started to come by, dropping by unannounced to look for Dad. He was quite young and had a wonderful smile. Dad was angry that he kept coming by, and I think he resented the fact that Gary liked his kids. One of the last times I saw him, he gave Thomas and me classic books for our tenth birthday. Mine was *Little Women* by Louisa M. Alcott. He'd inscribed the inside cover page, "Dec., 1972, for Dawn with love, Gary." Dad must have spoken to him because he soon stopped coming by altogether. The last time I saw him, he was working at a men's clothing shop in downtown Toronto. Later, I learned that Gary died of AIDS at the age of forty-two.

When school was out, Dad decided to rip out the old coal furnace and dig up the basement floor. Workmen came in with jackhammers. A digger removed debris and deepened the foundation. Then a cement truck came by and poured concrete through the small, side basement window. Watching all of this in amazement, I accidentally dropped a dill pickle into the freshly poured cement. It was removed and the men scowled at me as they had to smooth over the spot again.

When everything had dried, a new, smaller furnace was installed along with a wall to separate the laundry room from the rec room. Paneling with insulation went up around the outer walls of the room. Next, orange shag carpeting and a good-quality under pad were installed. I wondered what was going on and why Dad was going to all this trouble just to fix up the basement. Well, the answer came soon enough.

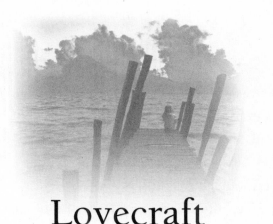

Lovecraft

S teve officially moved into the newly renovated rec room that autumn when I was eight. I morbidly expected something awful to happen to him, but he continued living with us for the next four years. Though Dad and Steve lived under the same roof and in a way could have been said to be going steady, Dad reserved the right to mess around with other men whenever the fancy took him. Sometimes while Steve was dressing in the morning, I would go downstairs to watch him put on moisturizer, bronzer, cologne, and mascara, and even use an eyelash curler. His neatly aligned toiletries filled an entire shelf. I was surprised by how particular and familiar he was with these cosmetic details. I had never seen my mother put her face together in a morning ritual that compared to his. Sometimes during the quiet of the evening, he would pull out his oil paints and start working at an easel or show me other crafts with which he was experimenting. I was particularly taken by the colorful, bohemian-style prints by Henri de Toulouse-Lautrec that decorated his walls. And I was mystified to see that Steve's apartment was the repository for the sticks and straps with which Mom disciplined us. Why would he want those implements in his room?

Often Dad, Steve, Mom, and I would ride to Taylor Creek Park, but I still felt unsteady on my bike and would fall easily. Some Saturday afternoons, my brothers and I would travel there on our own, while other times, Steve and Dad went off alone without us. On winter nights, I went skating at Toronto's Nathan Phillips Square with Dad, Steve, or another of Dad's lovers, and sometimes Mom and my brothers. We'd skate to the sounds of both classical and pop music. Christmas lights and decorations festooned the lampposts and overhead walkways. For a break, we'd go over to the concession stand for watered-down, but very hot, chocolate that would burn the roof of my mouth for the first number of sips. After a few dozen laps on the rink, I would loosen the laces on my white figure skates to ease the strain on my ankles before going back onto the ice again. Though in a way these were family outings, Dad was fundamentally disinterested in his children, and almost none of his lovers had children of their own. Even though they might take a passing interest in me, these men, I knew, were not interested in me personally except as a way to get closer to Dad.

Dad took me to Yorkville in the evenings to see the parts of the town being renovated. He was exhilarated about some of the cruising areas for gay men that had opened up. Dad liked his many partners and the nightlife downtown, and in my unknowing way, I absorbed his excitement. I would sit in the backseat with my head leaning back, staring up through the back window of the car as glowing office and apartment towers glided past. I had little idea what this was all about, except men were standing around looking at each other on both sides of the street outside the cafés and storefronts. Sometimes during the day, Dad would take me to the downtown gay village where artists sold their wares and introduce me to men he knew. As well, Dad took me to the sophisticated designer shopping district and some of the finer restaurants. He let me know that there was a particular apartment building that I was not allowed to visit where he sometimes stayed overnight with his friends. Sometimes Dad took all three of his kids to Woodbine Beach Pools, ostensibly for a family swim. Once we arrived, he would ditch us at the pool with strict instructions not to go any-where, dive off the high diving board, or talk to strangers, while he went off to search for fresh sexual conquests. We didn't know where he went on those occasions, but we were instructed not to call any attention to ourselves in case other adults noticed these three kids out for the day without an adult chaperone.

Over meals at our kitchen table, I often heard Dad talk about the gay bathhouses. These steamy establishments were places where gay or bisexual men could meet to have anonymous sex in downtown Toronto. They often got raided by the police and closed down, but they would soon reopen farther along Yonge Street or on one of the nearby side streets. While Dad never took me to the bathhouses, he did introduce me to Hanlan's Point. This was the unofficial "gay beach" at the more secluded end of Toronto Island, where men often would meet and pair off together to talk and pos-sibly have sex in the sections of tall grass. Other areas were more hidden from view. Though it was illegal, lots of nude sunbathing went on there, and people would tip off each other at first sight of the police. Dad scouted out the best areas of the beach before we set down our blanket, and I wondered why he'd brought me along. I didn't see any other children around at all. Was I being used as some kind of bait? Would the presence of a child appeal to the type of man with whom he was hoping to score? Just before sunset, Dad asked me to remove all my clothes to go swimming, but I adamantly refused, much to his disappointment.

Being around Dad increased my conflicting feelings of curiosity, guilt, and confusion about sex. Sex was nothing special to him. He regarded it as something gratuitous, but instinctively I did not and never would. Late on Friday nights when I had my own bedroom, I would flip through the few channels on my TV and come upon some pornographic programming on CITY TV. It was hard to look away, but if I heard footsteps coming down the hall, I switched it off. A few years later when I was with my father at CITY TV's downtown broadcast center, I overheard him say to the staff, "Glad you brought back the *Baby Blues*. I like watching it." Dad was a staunch supporter of freedom of sexual expression and had even done some modeling for underground magazines and pornography.

One particular day, Dad and his boyfriend du jour took me into a classy fashion district in Yorkville to check out a new underwear shop for men, where I was thoroughly grossed out by some of the form-fitted designs and flat-out frontal exposure depicted on posters and mannequins. Dad took me along to the meeting places of all the various gay subcultures—the cruising parks and neighborhoods, the clubs, and the beaches. Dad enjoyed the cosmopolitan ambience that surrounded him and his friends, and he wanted to share it with me. Imagine, a farm boy living this lifestyle! His eyes were always searching for more to have and to hold, while I was just searching for his secure love. I was afraid of being discarded like so many of his partners if I dared utter an unthankful word, so I did not disturb his fantasy. I would go out with him almost anywhere, always hoping he would notice and value me for who I was.

Sometimes walking along with Dad and his boyfriend after work during the summer, I would struggle to keep up with them. He would take me to fine restaurants where men could pick up each other. I noticed the acceptance, the smiling, and the easy sense of fun inside these places. Often, there was a mixed crowd of straight couples, visiting tourists, and gay men who seemed to live in the area. I didn't realize at the time all that was going on. It was important to be with Dad despite the degrading environments to which I was being introduced and desensitized. You take for granted what becomes an everyday occurrence. If you hear it and see it enough, you believe it and accept it as convention.

He explained how the hippies and flower children had lived in the Yorkville area and how it was being revitalized. One night, he took me into Lovecraft, a sex shop that had just opened in the early seventies. I remember the cluttered displays of fruit-flavored lotions, skin-tone dildos, edible panties, adult sex games, and lingerie. I felt a bit young to be seeing all this, but Dad didn't look at sexual things that way. He coaxed my curiosity about sex and encouraged me to have a look at the new gadgets as I innocently picked up huge vibrators and dildos, wondering how they were used. Perhaps sensing how inappropriate this might appear to others, he would lean over and ask me to put down a dildo when he noticed a salesclerk coming our way. Mom would quietly stand outside the store while Dad and I were inside. "She needs to know about sex," he told her.

Dad took me along the sidewalks to meet the artists and crafts people selling their wares. He would recognize some of the entrepreneurs and chat with them for a bit and then move on. One of Dad's boyfriends brought home a carved wooden man in a barrel and when you lifted up the barrel, an erect wooden phallus popped out. Some of his friends painted and sculpted, using various media to depict a number of subjects and themes but with a preponderance of sexual imagery. There was one tacky painting that you had to look at in different shades of light to get the whole effect. When you passed the painting from light to shadowy darkness, you would see two naked men in a sexual position. The thick oil colors were in shades of brown and black and looked almost as though human feces had been used to paint the figures.

During a visit to Montreal with Dad when I was sixteen, he decked me out in special lilac and purple "Bloomies'" panties he had purchased for me on one of his trips to New York and some shiny, white, see-through short shorts with slits up the sides. We parted for a while downtown as he went off to some assignation, and I was instructed to later walk back to the Ritz Hotel, where I would meet him for supper. Within a few minutes I was groped by a young man on a bicycle and was then mistaken for a prostitute by an older geezer who took hold of my backside. Looking down at myself, I realized with shamed surprise that Dad had completely manipulated and used me. He had induced me into looking like a hooker, believing I was too uptight about sex.

When I was eight, Mom and Dad decided I was old enough to have my own room. Dad painted the walls a bright lavender color that delightfully changed the whole ambience of the room. Up until then, I had always shared the middle bedroom with my brothers. I was ecstatic to finally have some privacy for the first time in my life. Dad bought me a spherical mood lamp that reflected a multi-colored haze onto the walls at night, and one of his friends who was moving gave us some dresser drawers and other furniture accessories, which my brothers and I shared. For my first winter in my own haven, I decorated the two big panels in my window with an aerosol can of snow. Mother was not impressed.

Sometimes one of Dad's boyfriends would come over and help with decorating the house. One particular weekend, bold-striped black and gold wallpaper went up along the staircase and hallway walls. I disliked it, but that didn't matter. Before long, a fox hunt print in a gaudy, gold frame was placed above the mahogany desk in the living room where I did my homework. Dad went antiquing in search of silver and brass accent items and other miscellaneous trinkets from old barns and run-down shops in the country. Mirrors began to be placed in strategic places, and two faux marble tables with ornate lamps turned up in our living room, looking like what you might see in the lobby of a cheap but pretentious hotel.

That autumn, we also got our first black and white television set. When my parents and Dad's boyfriend du jour went out, my brothers and I would huddle up and watch TV while munching on salty, buttered popcorn. We were told not to go upstairs, not to turn on any lights, not to answer the phone, and not to open the door to anyone. This was another precaution our negligent parents undertook so busybody neighbors wouldn't know we were being left unsupervised.

Sometimes Dad forced me to watch television programming of a violent and sexual nature. Dad sat down with me in the newly renovated rec room and insisted that I watch a movie about Jack the Ripper who killed prostitutes and then sliced them up with a knife. Later, he had me watch a movie about the Boston Strangler. I was deeply disturbed by both these movies, but I couldn't talk to him about it. He reserved the right to tear down boundaries, overstepping my will for his.

Dad soon took on yet another job for a U.S.-based convenience retailing organization that had just entered the Canadian market. He recruited potential franchise operators for this chain for a few years, and then moved on to a successful executive recruiting company for a short stint as well. He was quite eager and ambitious and would stop at nothing to get to the top of his field. This seemed to improve our financial situation quite a bit, and he purchased a Chrysler New Yorker, but most of the new spoils were not shared with the family.

Once Scott was enrolled in school, Mom went to work outside the house for a Provincial government agency that had good health and dental benefits. In addition to attending school, Thomas and I cleaned the house—dusted, vacuumed, and organized. We also watched Scott, bringing him to and from school every day. I cleaned the washrooms once a week and usually cooked supper on school days as well. Staples in my culinary repertoire included baked chicken and potatoes, Hamburger Helper with ground beef, and boiled carrots or green beans. Then we would clean up the dishes and pots, drying them on the counter. We would cut the lawn on weekends, and we also had our jobs of peddling cleaning and paper products door to door.

Even though the kids were taking on more chores, Mom was feeling particularly overwhelmed by her re-entry into the work force and actually threatened at one point to place us all in an orphanage if we misbehaved. No matter how perfect I tried to be, I always made mistakes that caused me to get spanked or yelled at. Worse than the quickly administered punishments was the agony of having to wait for a beating. Once, when we were nine, we were told to strip naked and wait in the basement for our punishment, standing side by side facing the steps. We had been instructed twice not to walk on the lawn as it had just been fertilized, and Dad would be furious if he saw foot impressions in the grass. Even though beatings were routinely administered two or three times a week, this one stood out. As we waited in absolute humiliation—naked, cold, and shivering—Mom came down the steps and greeted us with a sneer. I had to lean over a small table as she struck me fifteen times with the narrow stick. I counted each strike to keep my mind off the humiliating pain. I was so sore and upset that I wept very hard and told Mom I hated her. This netted me another beating right away. I couldn't sleep on my back or sit in a chair for a number of days without the pain shooting up my entire body from the bruising and welts.

The beatings continued regularly until I was fourteen years old. Sometimes she'd beat me and then order me to perform some demeaning household chore, like cleaning all the toilets. The last time Mom was about to hit me, something inside of me snapped. Without any premeditation, I turned on her and kicked her square and hard right between the legs. I told her never to lay a hand on me again. She didn't. I hated doing that, but I felt like I had to protect myself.

Although Mom finally backed off in the discipline department after I struck back at her, Dad steadily became more invasive and weird. One sunny Saturday afternoon, he came up the stairs and called me over. He had a gleam in his eyes like he had some sort of plan or game to play on me. I hesitantly went over and stood beside him. He pulled me into a Rhett Butler-style embrace and kissed me on the mouth, pushing his tongue through to the back of my throat. A couple of years later, he fondled my breasts as he passed me in the hall. When I screamed, "Dad, don't do that!" he just grinned and walked away. Mom heard us but didn't think anything of it. She later said that she thought I was just overreacting. Another time, Dad grabbed and squeezed my breasts, saying, "I thought you weren't wearing a bra."

All I ever wanted was pure fatherly affection—a simple kiss on the cheek and a reassuring hug. If he ever gave me such proper attention, I don't remember it. Instead, all affection—if affection is what motivated such assaults—was sexualized, leaving me feeling humiliated, dirty, and somehow ashamed.

More sinister yet was his appalling cruelty to two neighborhood cats. These young cats would walk up and down our fence and drop into our backyard right next to the patio and our back door. It was a nuisance to Dad, who hated the smell of cat urine. He'd asked the neighbors to keep their cats out of our yard, but what were they supposed to do? Put them on leashes? One particularly pungent day in late spring, Dad had had enough and grabbed both cats and called me to come with him down to the rec room. Obediently but fearfully I followed him downstairs as he called for Mom to bring down her insulin bottle and a syringe. He asked about her daily dose as he calculated the fatal dose for the cats. I was too terrified to move as he asked me to stay and watch. He took the syringe filled with insulin and stuck it in each of the cats' hind legs, then watched for any reaction. We waited as the minutes ticked away.

One cat started screeching and running all over the room, and Dad grabbed it and gave it another injection to quiet it down. The other cat just got dopey and finally still. My breathing was so shallow I became lightheaded, but I didn't want Dad to know how terrified I was as the smell of insulin filled the room.

Dad asked for a green garbage bag in which to place the cats and then dumped them in the metal garbage pail just outside the back door. How could he do such a thing? Sure, he grew up on a farm where animals were euthanized when they were sick and were slaughtered routinely for food. But surely he realized that this was different. That was supposed to be the end of the cat problem, but they weren't dead. The next morning we heard them still mewing. Dad didn't expect anything could live after injecting so much insulin into them. Perhaps a little sickened by the whole operation, he ordered Mom to drive the squirming, mewing bag to another neighborhood where garbage was being picked up that day. I was sent out with her as she carried out this atrocious deed and was warned never to tell anyone about it or all kinds of awful things would happen to me.

Dad's growing boldness as a homosexual was notable at this point. This was partly due to the fact that he was now earning good money and there was no one around to whom he felt he had to answer in terms of how he conducted his life. But there was also a new permissiveness permeating society. Though openly gay sitcoms, plays, pop stars and twenty-four-hour gay TV networks were still a few decades away, the early seventies was the period when gay themes started to turn up in the broader mainstream culture.

I remember Dad poring over the ads in the movie section of the *Toronto Star* for the film of Gore Vidal's satire about a sex change operation, *Myra Breckinridge*. Looking over his shoulder, I was transfixed by the photograph of Mae West that appeared in the ad. Then almost eighty years old, this bosomy battleship with dimming bedroom eyes was coasting into her final harbor, still dispensing her trademark double entendres and smutty wisecracks.

More locally, Dad was a huge fan of female impersonator Craig Russell, whose repertoire of characters was a who's who of the sort of tough and oversized women on steroids who speak to the gay male soul. Decked out in wigs, makeup, and elaborate costumes, Russell did an uncanny job of assuming the personae of such singing and acting stars as Judy Garland, Carol Channing, Bette Davis, Mae West, Barbra Streisand, Tallulah Bankhead, Marlene Dietrich, and Peggy Lee. He performed his impersonations all over the United States and Europe. Equally remarkable as the range of his characterizations was Russell's three-octave voice that allowed him to flawlessly impersonate Barbra Streisand in her own key. In 1990, Craig Russell died of an AIDS-related stroke at the age of forty-two.

Around this same time, Dad took me to a Kathryn Kuhlman healing crusade at the O'Keefe Center in Toronto. It was standing room only as we leaned against a wall of the auditorium to take in the slightly unsettling spectacle of this woman in a flowing gown with a hyperventilating voice, driving satanic spirits out of her subjects. Why did Dad want me to see her? Dad never would abandon completely the Christianity of his youth. One morning, I asked him a moral question about heaven and hell, and he put a black, leather-bound Bible into my hands, saying, "This is where you'll find truth." Even if it was only remnant legalism left over from his youth, how did his continued regard for the Christian faith jibe with the appallingly sinful life he was leading? Part of it was a matter of "Do as I say, not as I do." Even though Dad could hardly keep his pants on, I wasn't allowed to wear anything but dresses and skirts until my grade five gym teacher sent home a note saying pants were mandatory. I couldn't understand why Dad could do all the sexual stuff he did and I couldn't dance or wear makeup. Certain music was not allowed in the house either, because of its rock beat or lyrics. Yet Dad listened to whatever kind of revved up devil music he liked. While Christianity obviously still exerted a pull on my father, the church to which he most completely belonged was the church of phallic eroticism. Fitfully try as he might to adhere to a Christian creed, he was more hooked into the kinds of sexual behaviors that glorified that randy little god. Watching that campy evangelist that Sunday, I couldn't help but suspect that part of Kuhlman's appeal for him was the almost grotesque parody of femininity that she embodied. With a few minutes of mugging in front of his mirror, I'm sure Craig Russell could easily have added Kuhlman to his cast of brassy dames writ large.

It took me a long time to understand why I never could be the apple of my father's eye. But there were always inverted men and overblown women who did a better job of realizing my father's distorted feminine ideals than I ever could, who were more grown up, sophisticated, and perfect. I felt small in comparison to these gifted men and masculine women who exhibited all the desirable traits to which my father was drawn in a woman and who were outrageously famous, rich, and beautiful to boot.

Erratic Provision

Steve had a little cottage in St. Catharines that belonged to his mother, where he invited us all to stay. Sleeping there alone in a guest bedroom the first night, my front felt painfully tender. I was just beginning the early stages of puberty at age nine and becoming more aware of my own body. I was also beginning to understand in a way that I couldn't articulate just what it meant for all of us—me, my brothers, and my mother—that Dad preferred to have sex with other men.

There was a screened-in porch behind the cottage with a double bed in it. Thomas and I got to sleep out there one night during a thunderstorm. I so enjoyed the strong, cool breeze before the storm, the sound of the moving water below hitting the eroded shoreline, and the dark clouds enshrouding the moonlight. Dad was out with Steve, so Mom, my brothers, and I were alone during the storm.

Mom just came along on any trip, including this one, at Dad's request, even though his boyfriends were present. She did not complain about Dad being out late with Steve, checking out the downtown nightlife. But I knew she was hurt and humiliated and felt hopelessly entangled in this relationship with this defector of a husband and father. Though her temper was short and she was too distracted to pay much attention to her children, mostly she was ominously silent.

The morning after the storm, Dad showed up all giddy and smiling with Steve after being out all night. We piled into the long silver-gray Chrysler for a drive over to the miniature golf course. It was my first time wielding a putter, and my hands felt unsteady as I tried to follow Dad's directions. Some of my shots flew way out of bounds, but others somehow made it into the hole. There were enough of these that I actually won a free game. I played the second round, initially hoping that I could win a third game, but my interest quickly flagged along with my performance.

One morning, Steve's mother unexpectedly arrived and found us in her cottage while I was on my hands and knees, scrubbing the floor in the kitchen. She yelled at us to get out, which wasn't at all what I expected. Here I was cleaning up her cottage as Mom had instructed, and she was not appreciating my work. It was embarrassing, but within a few minutes she reappeared and said we could stay. She was angry with her son for not telling her we'd be there but recognized that she had been terribly rude to us. While she probably knew what was going on between Dad and Steve, I suspect she lost her cool when she realized a wife and children were being impacted by all this as well. To make up for this, she invited Mom and me to a country club garden party later that afternoon.

When we got home from the cottage, Dad wanted us to get some color on our white Northern European skin and instructed Mom and me to get tans. So we started sunbathing in the backyard on our pink-tiled patio next to our piddly lawn and garden. We applied a special cream that darkened the tan faster. I couldn't believe that by just lying on my back and blissfully absorbing the sun's rays, I could please my taskmaster father. I actually got to relax for a few days that summer.

As providers, my parents were, to say the least, erratic. They made no plans for our post-secondary education, but Thomas and I were enrolled in Cub Scouts and Brownies. Mother took us to special programs like the Ice Capades, the circus, orchestra concerts, and children's plays, and Thomas and I took piano lessons. We also attended a performance of *Madame Butterfly* through school. Dad sometimes took us to Santa Claus parades in Toronto. Later in my early teens, he teasingly mentioned the time and location of the first Gay Pride Parade but then admonished us not to go. So of course we went to check it out, standing across the street from a members-only gay bar: St. Charles Tavern. While looking for Dad and his boyfriend, and believing he was withholding valuable details from us, we watched drag queens waltz up Yonge Street.

While my parents had seen to it that I was outfitted with glasses as well as braces for my teeth, similar attention was not paid to Scott. No one was supervising his hygiene, and when he was finally taken to the dentist when he was about ten, he had a mouthful of cavities. I did not always have a winter coat, so I often wore an undershirt, blouse, and sweater with a spring overcoat during the winter months. Sometimes my skirts were indecently short. I felt ashamed that I didn't have nice clothes to wear to school. Bullies would surround me sometimes and pull at my clothes to expose my underclothes. They would slap my face, trip me to the ground, and pull my hair. I hardly ever resisted, as it only made things worse when I tried to fight back. The teachers and principal never really protected me until one day in grade five.

That day, about ten kids stood around as I was being slapped and punched, with my dress held up over my head. The children were saying, "Pull down her underwear." In the midst of this humiliation, a thirteen-year-old boy stepped forward and told them to stop, making the kids scatter. His name was Peter. He had curly blond hair, fair skin, and blue eyes. I was grateful that someone thought enough of me to defend me from this mob of bullies.

On a winter day that same year, I looked to the street beyond the school's black iron fence and saw a man dancing up and down with his pants at his knees. I was so frightened that it took me a few moments to go find someone with whom to talk. I told a girlfriend who was in the next grade, and she and I went to the principal's office together. I could not identify the man, but it was then that I was able to report the horrible experiences I'd endured in the schoolyard during recess and after school. I identified each of the culprits to the principal while looking through class pictures. These kids were then called down to his office and given a talk. I was afraid that I might be beaten up in retaliation, but the principal assured me that this would not happen and it didn't. Nothing that bad ever happened again.

From that winter day forward, Peter often would walk me home along with his younger sisters to keep me feeling safe. He didn't say much. He wasn't a very articulate fellow, and I don't think he did too well in school. He had far too much responsibility for a thirteen-year-old boy. Once, after walking over the railway tracks and taking some shortcuts, I passed by his house and looked in, only to find it unkempt and barely furnished. His mother was often in a drunken stupor, leaving Peter to take care of his younger siblings. Obviously, there was no father on the scene. It was wonderful to think that someone from so harsh a background had so well developed a sense of justice and fairness that he would put his neck out for someone he scarcely knew. The following September, I stood in the schoolyard waiting to see him and his sisters, as I'd missed them through the summer. But I never saw him again.

I had just turned ten. One night, Dad came home from work and announced we were going to drive to Florida immediately. We didn't have any suitable luggage, so clothes were thrown into garbage bags and tossed into the trunk. Steve sat in the front seat between Dad, who was driving, and Mom. I assumed he was there to share driving duties. The Chrysler New Yorker was long and roomy inside, so my brothers and I and our new Chihuahua, Skipper, could sleep with our pillows on either the back seat or the carpeted floor just behind the front seat. We were excited and noisy but eventually fell asleep as the car traveled through the dark American night, stopping now and then for gas and a bite to eat.

It was Holiday Inn for breakfast, McDonald's for lunch, and Kentucky Fried Chicken for supper. Driving through Kentucky, I was struck by the beauty of the green rolling hills and winding roads. While I appreciated the landscape, Dad had an eye for passing fashion accessories. Approaching a gas station, Dad called out, "Look at that guy's cowboy boots!" He was particularly taken with the shiny brass spurs hooked on the back. Dad pulled in there, and we tumbled out of the car to grab some refreshments for the next leg of the journey. Thomas was instructed to tie the long, roped leash to the back door on the driver's side so Skipper could get some fresh air and a pathetic semblance of exercise.

After filling up, we all scrambled back into the car and had pulled on to the gravel on-ramp when we heard frantic high-pitched howls from the back. We looked around and saw Skipper flying up and down behind the vehicle, hitting the gravel again and again. Dad told Steve to slow down gradually so Skipper wouldn't roll under the wheels of the braking car. Steve slowed down and within seconds the car came to a halt. Skipper was lying on his side with skinned, bleeding paws, chest, and hind legs, and seemed to be breathing with difficulty. Dad gently picked up Skipper, wrapped him in a towel and laid him on my mother's lap as we drove off in search of an animal hospital.

We found a country veterinarian open, and Skipper was ushered quickly into the office where his condition was assessed. Dad had become quite pale and was pacing the floor until the doctor insisted he was in shock and should sit down immediately. Dad hesitantly concurred and was given some medication to calm him. By the time we saw Skipper, he'd been bandaged up like a four-legged mummy and heavily sedated with pain relievers. I wondered if he'd survive, but we were assured he'd make it though what easily could have been the end.

As we entered Florida, we saw a huge welcoming sign that spanned the entire roadway. To mark our arrival in Lotus Land, we immediately stopped at an orange grove and each had a real orange to eat. It was juicy, sweet, and fresh—nothing like the oranges from the supermarket up in Canada. Later that day, we went off to our motel where we would be staying for the week. It was a pokey rectangular room with a small kitchen in the corner that became hotter and hotter as the air stagnated. The inadequate glass windowpanes were horizontally hinged and could be rolled outward to let in a hint of fresh air. While Dad was out gallivanting with Steve, Thomas cracked his head open while playing outside, and Mom had to take him to the nearest hospital by taxi. When Dad came back, he was seriously ticked off and actually blamed Thomas for injuring himself.

Next door to us were some boys from Ohio. They always played with my brothers and me, and if it weren't for them, we wouldn't have had much fun. Dad went out cruising most nights with Steve, while Mom and us children stayed in and around the motel. It was not your typical family vacation. Mom and I were not very happy with this arrangement. First of all, we had no vehicle when Dad and Steve were gone, so we had to hang around the motel most of the time, making meals and cleaning up afterward. Dad would come back with Steve, who would pay us off with Mars Bars if we had done all of our chores. We did visit Walt Disney World in Orlando one day and Cypress Gardens another day. But otherwise this vacation was strictly for Dad and Steve, and the rest of us were nothing more than accident-prone pests who happened to be along for the ride.

Dad was now earning enough money to set his sights on the more posh neighborhoods of Toronto like Rosedale and Forest Hill. He'd become a successful executive recruiter for a big firm and was running a franchise recruiting operation in the old business district along King Street. He also owned shares in other branches of the firm that he'd shrewdly scooped up when the past president fell ill. For all the flamboyance and risk-taking of his personal life, as a businessman Dad was a thoroughgoing conservative. He disliked gay men who were queens or exhibited feminine airs, and there wasn't a hint of any of that in his professional demeanor.

Finally, we moved to a wealthy Jewish neighborhood in Forest Hill, where we had a much bigger yard and garden than we'd ever had before. Shortly after moving in, Dad built me a tree house out there. My brothers and I were whisked away to church camp for a week, while my parents and Steve did some redecorating in the kitchen, wallpapering, carpeting, and painting the cupboards white with black trim. Colorful husks of Indian corn, ivory linen curtains, and Norman Rockwell prints accessorized the kitchen walls. The Rockwell painting of a cheerful, ruddy-faced family huddled together around a table for their Thanksgiving feast represented an ideal that nobody in our family had ever known. Not only did we almost never sit together to eat, most nights of the week we didn't even sleep under the same roof.

Our new home was closer to Dad's second residence that he'd shared with Steve and a string of other boyfriends for the last couple of years. Though this apartment was only about ten blocks away from us, we were told to never come by. One day Thomas, in the grip of some pressing concern, disregarded that prohibition and went to see his dad. In a state of annoyance, Dad opened the door, saw who it was, and wordlessly closed it, as if Thomas was nothing more to him than some pesky door-to-door salesman. Going round to the back of the house and peeping through a bedroom window, Thomas witnessed my father having group sex with about a dozen other men. Sometimes we'd overheard him talking about such trysts on the phone, but seeing one was even more disturbing. Thomas struggled with the trauma of this sighting for a long time, looking through some of Dad's gay pornography even though the images repelled him, and wondering why Dad could kiss other men— strangers even—but never express affection to his own son.

Though we weren't to visit Dad's house, he could drop in on us any time he liked—erratically through the week and more often on the weekends when he might fix a few things or take care of the yard and expect his wife and kids to wait on him.

I often would babysit for a dollar or two per hour on Friday and Saturday nights and not get home until after two in the morning. Yet Dad still would wake me up at seven by yanking open my bedroom curtains and saying, "Get up. There's work to be done. You can't just sleep there all day like a lazy cow." Dad would ask me to take afternoon tea to him in the backyard, using either our white everyday china or sometimes the full silver tea service. He'd always want snacks like chips and dip, raw rhubarb with salt, or fresh veggies and dip later in the afternoon. Then I'd have to help make supper, which often would be baked potatoes with barbecued chicken or steak, corn on the cob, and freshly ripened red tomatoes from the back garden. After shopping with Mom in the morning, I still could be working into the evening, cleaning up the dishes and barbecue utensils. I quickly learned to avoid this by staying away on the weekends when he was home. When I got a little older, I sometimes tried not coming home at all except for the later evenings when he'd usually be out with his boyfriends.

Dad didn't know and might not have cared that Mom didn't come home some nights either. There wasn't much left in my parents' relationship by this point. They hadn't resumed sexual intercourse after Scott was born. One night, Dad shared with me how he really didn't like our mother and wished he'd never married her. He told me he was more comfortable around men. Though he didn't give a name for it, I understood what he meant. I wanted to express some compassion for him, but I couldn't. I saw this condition of his as an act of betrayal that had destroyed any possibility of happiness for everyone in our family. On those nights when he did come home, Dad slept in the attic bedroom that was built the first autumn we moved in.

Increasingly Mom was off in her own world too—a rather desperate world of ballroom dancing, facelifts, and far-fetched dreams of becoming a model. I believe the facelifts were another form of submission to Dad's need to have youth and beauty surrounding him, attracting his joy boys. Mom's need for superficial affection was met when the male dancers at the studio would embrace her during the waltzes and whisper pretty things in her ear, making her feel beautiful. She often went out with girlfriends and later on used an expensive dating service.

For our next family outing from hell, Dad took us to Niagara Falls, where he rendezvoused with yet another lover. On an afternoon's outing well above the falls, Dad, dressed in frayed jean shorts with a shirt wrapped about his neck, was in one of his reckless, risk-taking moods. He took us to a narrow part of a watercourse, possibly a creek. "Horseshoe Falls is just down the river from us," he said. He crossed the rapidly flowing watercourse from one side to the other, securing a rope around the trunk of a small tree as a lifeline on to which we could all hold as we crossed after him. He insisted that we all had to follow. The water tugged at my legs, and had it not been for the rope, I could have lost my balance and been swept away by the strong current. I was especially concerned for Scott, who didn't have as much ballast as the rest of us. We finally made it across but not without eliciting a lot of gasps from the audience of women on the other side who stood there aghast at my father for taking such a risk with his children and our mother.

Later, just Dad and I went farther down to the edge of a cliff with a steep drop below it. There was a large rocky area that was five feet or so across from where we stood. He jumped over first and then reached out his hand to have me jump over to join him. I hesitated. This was another of those, "Will you come with me to the end of the pier?" moments when I realized that I fundamentally didn't trust this man. "Why do I have to go over there?" I asked. "I just want to stay where I am." He called me a sissy name and held out his hand. I told him I was afraid, but he kept pressuring me. Against my better judgment, almost in a spirit of bullheadedness, I leapt across the chasm. Grabbing hold of his hand, I feared for a second that I might pull both of us down, but he pulled me sprawling onto the rock. And for what? The scenery wasn't any better on the other side. I stood with Dad for only a moment and, thinking my fragile courage might dissolve further if I waited much longer, said, "I want to go back." He jumped first and then reached out his hand to assist me back over to the grassy land by the cliff. I never understood why he did this or what his motivations were, but I remembered a newly written family insurance policy that he'd bragged about before the trip. It's hard not to suspect that he was at least toying with the idea of cashing in.

My brothers and I tried to fit in with a few of our neighbors but didn't make much headway. After a few summers, we realized we never would be readily accepted in this Jewish enclave. This wasn't just a religious difference; it was sociological as well. I made a few casual friends my own age, but the older crowd never took to us. Jewish friends, whether conservative or reform, had parents who were very involved in their lives, expecting university education and good paying jobs in their children's futures. Their parents invested a lot of time and resources in their progeny, making sure they had the right kind of clothes and social experiences that would ensure bright futures with lots of grandchildren. These well-meaning moms and dads lived for their children and took them to the cottage and on trips together (without a spare joy boy in tow) and didn't make them work all the time serving them at barbecues. Compared to them, our family ethos was nonexistent. Non-Jewish neighbors beyond a six-block radius of our house were a little more welcoming, but all in all, our years in Forest Hill were years in exile.

Not that my parents were ever mixers or kept in touch with a circle of friends. No stable couples—with or without children—ever visited our home. But even though he had precious little to do with our neighbors socially, Dad did everything he could to uphold property values. He started coming home more on weekends and took an interest in decorating the place, bringing in plants, antiques, and brass and silver accent articles. Orange carpet was installed in the living and dining room areas along with expensive mahogany furniture. Mirrors with gaudy gold-leaf edges went up on the walls at the top and bottom of the stairwell. He had a friend paint the main washroom a brilliant dark blue. He stained the hallway floor and stairs, redid all the wiring, and had all the closets refitted with new doors. The rec room was repainted dark brown and decorated with painted wooden shutters instead of curtains. He kept the dining room's corner liquor cabinet well stocked with all the latest labels, and my baby brother began sneaking small amounts. When he was about ten, I watched Scott knock back a whole shot of vodka in one gulp on a dare.

When black refugees moved into a subsidized apartment build-ing at the top of the street, Dad was worried real estate values would drop. After neighbors expressed similar concerns, the refugees moved out. Hoping to discourage anyone else from moving into those properties, Dad goaded Scott to break their windows and steal the telephones. This only pushed Scott further into the sort of delinquent behavior with which he was already experimenting. He started stealing jewelry from his friends' homes, stealing money from cloakrooms, and hanging with the wrong crowd. His school performance suffered severely as well, and not just academically. Scott got into a lot of fights. He didn't eat well and often slept at other people's homes. Even at three, Scott had run away and was found hours later at a doughnut shop, sitting with a police officer who plied him with hot chocolate and pastries. Scott really needed a fatherly hand to guide him at about this point, but Dad spent even less time with Scott than he had with me. I never remember seeing Dad talk with Scott at all, except to bark at him to clean up his room.

After years of too strict control, my distracted parents were now backing away from the job of parenting almost completely. While I welcomed the lifting of the embargo against buying records, oth-erwise I felt like I was being cut adrift. Socially I was left to fend for myself. Bedtimes and curfews became a thing of the past on weekends, and I was free to come and go pretty much as I pleased. The only problem was, I didn't have a clue about what sort of in-teraction with my peers would please me.

I questioned my sexual identity and second-guessed all my friendships. Living in such an uncertain family situation, I assumed and dreaded that I would have to experiment sexually to discover what my identity was. I felt uncomfortable and ambivalent in the company of female friends and couldn't relate to their easy chatter about boys, shopping, teachers, and summer vacations. I didn't seem to live in the same world as these girls—just their neighborhood. The only time I could ever relax and be myself was in the company of a few boys who'd made it clear their interest in me was strictly platonic. I didn't bond with boys or girls during my teens; I saw everyone as transient, not unlike my father's relationships in the subcultures. With Dad there was, of course, no winning. If I hung out with girls, he'd call me "dyke" or "lesbo." If I hung out with boys, he called me "whore."

It was easier at times to act as if I were promiscuous, pretending to be at ease sexually among boys even though I wasn't. Promiscuity seemed to be the normal thing to me. It was what I saw in the movies and what my father had constantly modeled, but it wasn't something I wanted any part of. I was hungry for affection and warmth, a little cuddling perhaps, but romantically or sexually, I didn't know what I wanted or if I wanted anything. It didn't help that around this time our family physician was encouraging me to be sexually active with boys as soon as possible to make sure I didn't turn out like my father. Not only did he encourage me to have intercourse, he told me how a few of his young female patients were having sex with him in his car. Was I supposed to be impressed or want some of this action for myself? When I was twenty-one and having a planter's wart removed from my foot, these overtures went from suggestive to overt. As I was wobbling about on my freshly treated foot getting ready to leave, he cornered me in the archway of his door, placed his arms around me, and drew me close to him, kissing me on the forehead. "This is a male-female thing," he said. Right then and there, I terminated our ten-year physician-patient thing.

On the morning of my thirteenth birthday I began menses. Struggling with painful cramps and a dizziness that I had never felt before, I stayed home from school. I called Mom at work for some consolation, and she told me to lie down and take it easy. After work, we walked to a Chinese restaurant to celebrate my birthday. Of course, Dad was nowhere in sight. On the way home, we picked up a K-Tel record with the latest pop rock tunes on it. I didn't have any hope for the future at this point in my life. I couldn't imagine ever getting married and had vowed never to have children at all. Occasionally, I would catch myself entertaining an innocent fantasy of being with a boy who loved me and sometimes would hold me. In my escape fantasy, the boy and I lived in a wooded area next to a pond in an unfurnished tree house where there were no insects or sex.

I was pretty sure I liked boys, or would someday, but I thought I was too ugly for anyone really to like me. Even at a size 8, I thought I was fat, and I had a poor self-image. I would become even skinnier by my late teens as I fretted about being overweight and half-starved myself. I habitually wore layered, shapeless clothing—blue jeans mostly—topped off with one of my father's or brother's shirts with the sleeves rolled up. The fabric was soft and flexible, and I felt somehow protected in a man's shirt. What one wore affected who accepted you, and I always had to be in control in my relationships with boys. That way, I could not be taken advantage of. I preferred friendships that were platonic, and most boys were hardwired to want more than that. I wanted freedom and independence from any kind of emotional neediness. I noticed how men did not face the same prejudices women did and were not treated like doormats so often. I could see advantages to being male, and sometimes wished I had been born a guy. Yet here I was in a very curvy feminine body and cover it up as I might, boys started to notice it and respond to it.

I was sitting up in my tree house one afternoon when a rather pushy boy named Daniel came up to visit me and, in hardly any time at all, slipped his arm around me. He was a bright kid from a broken home, intelligent with knowledge gleaned from traveling around the world. He knew how electricity worked and how to hook up stereo equipment. And he knew a fair bit about girls from his experiences in Israel at the time of his bar mitzvah. He was an intriguing guy, though I wasn't sure I liked him even from the start and was increasingly certain I didn't over the next few months as we drifted into a miserable one-sided relationship, with him always pushing for more and me holding back.

What was most unnerving about the wretched time we spent together was the way I would be coerced to take a few tentative steps down any romantic/sexual avenue with Daniel only to be confronted with one nauseating memory or another involving my father. Daniel wanted to French kiss? Yikes! Who was the first person who forced one of those on me? He wanted to fondle my breasts? Ditto. He wanted to impress me by showing me his collections of pornography and sex aids? Yep, been there, too. His only original touch was when it came to cruelty to animals. Daniel killed mice for sick sport, not cats.

Though Dad presented an unruffled appearance of confidence, intelligence, proficiency, and financial wellbeing to the world, he was fundamentally insecure. In many ways, he seemed as stubbornly wedged in the confusion of early adolescence as I was. He was never content with himself and was constantly trying to improve his appearance. He was often narcissistic, self-absorbed, and very needy for male affirmation and affection. He hardly could function at work or relax at home or on vacations without one of his boyfriends present. His ideal sexual partner was someone who would be very subordinate to his demands without being effeminate. He used power in these relationships, often with men ten years his junior. He needed both younger men and more powerful and influential men in his life and would idolize men who held more powerful positions in the business world.

He carried a lot of unresolved anger inside that boiled over in a way that often would silence and terrify those around him. There sometimes was violence between Dad and his sexual partners. He and his partners often berated their own friends and each other. It was strange hearing them exchange intolerant slurs about homosexuals and men who liked dressing as women. Dad and his friends had numerous and anonymous sexual partners and were involved in many different kinds of sexual behavior, including group sex. So, of course, there would be jealousy and hurt feelings from time to time as well as one-upmanship as each competed for attention. Then there was that legion of spurned ex-partners who would no longer come around.

Dad eventually broke up with Steve and brought different men around for us to approve or disapprove. He had been seeing different men while he was with Steve, and it wasn't as if any new partner would become a permanent fixture, so we really couldn't have cared less whom he chose. He eventually would settle on whomever he fancied for a little while, so why ask our opinion?

Though for a few months at a stretch it might appear Dad was settling into a monogamous relationship with just one other man, appearances were deceiving. In fact, Dad's sex life was becoming ever more chaotic and reckless.

He still had one-night stands with lovers he'd casually bring home on any night of the week or take to the new condo he'd just purchased on St. Charles Street in Toronto's gay village. Once again, we were not allowed to visit him there, but he reserved the right to drop in and out of our lives at will. Some nights, Dad would dress up and go out to the top of the street to be picked up by a friend for a night of cruising the gay districts downtown. Sometimes he took me along with him on these excursions. There were certain restaurants where gay or bisexual men could mingle openly and set up assignations. Business cards would be exchanged at the bar, or a waiter could discreetly deliver them between interested parties. Sometimes the waiter himself was the object of desire. One night, I watched Dad stroke a waiter's bum as our order was taken, with no one taking offense or thinking this was inappropriate. Dad often would strike up lewd conversations with men he'd just met, and before long I'd get the signal that it was time for me to disappear and leave them to it; perhaps meeting up later or just making my way home alone.

I sometimes wondered if there was a single homosexual in all of Metropolitan Toronto with whom Dad hadn't had sexual contact. I remember our brief transit down an escalator at a Bloor Street department store one night. Dad had just been lecturing me about the dangers of smoking (something I hadn't been doing or even contemplating) when his attention was otherwise seized. In the time it took us to descend one floor, Dad commented unfavorably about the male model on the poster to the left of us who was a horrible bore and spotted another of his conquests walking through the store. "That man has the worst case of scabies I've ever seen," Dad told me. *Ah, but I'll bet he doesn't smoke*, I thought.

In all of his relationships—professional, familial, extramarital—Dad often blamed others for not being good enough at something or for having the wrong perspective on things. He thought he was always right. Everyone else had the problem. This blame game went on for years before I understood why he had such a hard time taking personal responsibility for his own emotions and actions. I came to recognize that his own great and unmet need was the very same as mine. The absence of a loving father was the operative factor for both of us.

Dad had a hard time getting adequate rest, and thus took sleeping pills for many years. He also struggled fitfully with depression and at times thought about committing suicide. I overheard him saying he had chosen his latest condo because the windows didn't open onto a balcony off of which he might be tempted to jump. He lived a tortured life. As an adamant perfectionist, his way of coping was to bury himself in long, arduous shifts at the office and then escape through compulsive sexual activities in the evenings and on weekends. Idle moments were to be avoided, as those were the times when feelings of hopelessness and emptiness would come flooding in. In a life lived as frenetically as his, reflection—leading perhaps to remorse or reform—just wasn't a possibility. He was caught up in a vicious cycle of work and sexual addiction.

That spring, Dad told me the doctors had found something in his blood. This was something so unfamiliar that the doctors didn't even have a name for it yet, and they couldn't guarantee that he would live long. The only thing Dad could deduce was that it must be some type of rare cancer in the blood. He was frightened and anxious, and he shared these feelings with me. But this scare wasn't about to make him slow down the pace of his life. On the contrary, it impelled him to live faster than ever, desperate to cram in all of the fun and excitement he could.

It wasn't easy buying gifts for Dad, as he had now reached a place where he could afford just about anything he desired. I found a painting that year in a downtown gallery shop that I hoped he'd like. It depicted a sailboat on a calm body of water with a warm sunset bathing the entire scene. It was a beautiful image, evoking stillness and reflection, two qualities I thought Dad could fruitfully cultivate at this uncertain time in his life. The frame was nothing much, and Dad had it replaced with something of higher quality and more complementary to the image. But my instincts had been spot-on, and I was delighted when Dad set the painting in a prominent place beside his bedroom door.

Dad had been seeing a psychiatrist for the last few years; a trendy type, unfortunately, who was encouraging him to explore his sexuality. Newly threatened by the prospect of his own mortality, he listened more to this psychiatrist's voice than the quieter counsel of the painting I'd bought him. Dad threw himself into more and more risky sexual behaviors at an increased and even more frantic rate. As he tore his way through the gay bathhouses and racked up sexual partners beyond counting, he only seemed to become more belligerent and heedless of his impact on others. The desperate strategy he employed to keep the grim reaper at bay had in fact put down the welcome mat, and was inviting the cowled gent right into the darkest recesses of his bloodstream.

A Real Family

That summer, my brothers and I played at a nearby school-yard where we ran into Bryan, a boy with a Catholic background who was an agnostic. He was eighteen years old and over six feet tall with light blond hair and a thin, wiry build. Almost immediately, he began to come by the house nearly every day, playing and working with my brothers. Together they delivered newspapers, cut grass, and did yard and garden work for my father.

Bryan quickly forged a place of influence in my family. He was easily accepted by Dad, who liked having extra hands around to do yard work. Because he was that little bit older, stronger, and more experienced, Dad got Bryan to help with more difficult and complicated jobs around the house like waterproofing the foundation. Thankfully, sex wasn't an issue. Because Bryan wasn't his type (Dad preferred dark-haired men), he never got hit on even once. All of us, and especially Scott, enjoyed having Bryan around; he provided some of the much-needed attention we weren't getting from Dad. The strong relationship between Scott and Bryan would remain solid well into adulthood.

For a few years, Bryan played a pivotal role in my life as well. Bryan was there every day after school, providing me with conversation, insight, safety, and much-needed attention. No one before him had listened to me so well and asked so many probing questions about my life and experiences. With him I began to speak for the first time about the horrible and haunting secrets that had been locked up for so long in my mind. He invited me to go with him to baseball games, concerts, his friends' residences, and his apartment to spend time with his family.

Getting to know his family gave me a brand-new view of what family was supposed to be like: supportive, encouraging, and providing moral guidelines. Though Bryan only lived in a tiny two-bedroom apartment with his younger sister and his parents, this was a family that actually took care of each other. The parents welcomed their son's and daughter's friends into their home rather than pushing them away. I had never known this kind of home. Paying more attention to my physical needs than my own mother ever had and drawing on an income much smaller than my parents', Bryan's mother bought me a winter coat, mittens, a hat, a scarf, and sweaters. She was always there for me to talk to, and in her wise and caring counsel, she reminded me in some ways of Aunt Grace. She was incredulous when I told her that Mom and I spent five hours every Saturday on a shopping marathon for Dad. She knew Dad only wanted us out of the house so he could play with his joy boys, and she encouraged me to assert some independence and not go along with this absurd charade.

Bryan's father was a little more remote—a shy man of few words—but unfailingly kind and welcoming. His sister, Laura, was my age with red frizzy hair. She was a lot like her mother: kind and bluntly honest, yet always helpful. Once Laura pointed out to me that it was wrong to have two boyfriends at the same time. With my father's example before me, I actually had to think about that one for a moment but soon recognized the simple truth and decency of it. Of course, that was how it should be. In Laura's observant, well-grounded way, I suspect she knew long before I did that Bryan had developed deeper feelings for me. With the five-year age gap between us and the wonderful rapport he'd developed with my brothers, I wasn't picking up any such signals at all.

That winter, Bryan asked me to go for a walk with him early one evening. It had just snowed, and everywhere the heavy covering of snow sparkled from the light of the moon and the streetlights that shone down through the branches of the trees. It was a perfect night for lovers to take a walk. I frankly didn't know what love was. The feeling in my heart was wonderment that anyone would want to be with me or like the way I was dressed or want to take a walk and talk with me. Bryan made me feel special. He began to share his feelings about how he wanted me to be his girlfriend. I had no idea how to respond to him. It frightened me, and I shifted between wanting closeness and wanting to keep him at a distance—paralleling our relationship fumbles through a few break-ups and reunions over the next five years. Knowing about some of my experiences with Daniel, Bryan took care to not initiate sexual overtures at the beginning of our relationship and never forced sex on me at all.

Bryan became an everyday fixture in my life. He was as faithful and loyal as a St. Bernard, even on the days my hormones were surging and I frankly didn't want to see him. I couldn't fully appreciate, let alone receive, what he was feeling for me. The next summer, he asked for permission to hold me before I went in for the night and I told him yes. We were outside the side door of my house late at night. Leaning against the neighbor's wall and facing me, he gently pulled me into his embrace and kissed me. He seemed almost cautious, like he was holding back and not wanting to harm me or hurry me, but still I sensed his fevered attraction and even shared it to a degree. This simple kiss left me changed, giving me a precious first glimpse of how sweet love could be with the right person.

I had a guarded sort of security knowing Bryan wanted me to be in control of the physical part of our relationship and promised me he never would take advantage of me sexually. I was so needy for affection and attention that I welcomed the invitation even though I wasn't wildly in love with him. Always sensitive to my confused feelings around sexuality, Bryan gave me the space and time to figure out how I fit into the bigger world. If my feelings for him now are sad and conflicted, that is only because I know to this day that he gave me more than I ever gave him. I never returned his love in equal measure, and I regret that. It was unfair of me. But without the rock-solid circle of protection he provided, I don't know how I would have survived the storms of adolescence. No, I did not love him, but I will be forever in his debt.

Dad began seeing one boyfriend more regularly, but not exclusively, and started bringing Ron to our house. In addition to being Dad's main squeeze, Ron also worked at Dad's office as an accountant and sort of personal assistant. Ron moved right into our house most weekends and sometimes during the week, parking his baby-blue Volkswagen Beetle in the driveway and sleeping in Dad's attic bedroom. Ron was tall, dark haired, and thin—an appearance my father wished he had. He always dressed like a fashion model out of *GQ* magazine and was impeccably turned out no matter if he was in a business suit or casual clothes. He would help out with things around the house, such as installing new windows at the front and putting together bold "Hollywood" lights on my IKEA do-it-yourself bedroom dressing table. He did whatever Dad asked of him, and after their work they'd sit together out back sunbathing.

While I appreciated Ron's efforts on various household projects, mostly I resented him. Whenever he was around, at home or at the office (where I too was starting to do part-time work) there was no getting near Dad. Whenever I approached, Ron would head me off and ask me to leave the two of them alone. "Dawn, your father's busy with paperwork right now and mustn't be disturbed," he'd say.

We ignored each other most of the time and were stiffly cordial when we had to be. Occasionally, I'd be surprised when we managed to strike up a conversation of real interest.

In Dad's office one summer, Ron mentioned an electric facial sauna that he owned and how great it was at unclogging pores. I looked closely at his skin and sure enough, it had a wonderful glow to it. He used Clinique moisturizer and an expensive bronzer that never left streaks. He was much better at taking care of his appearance than I was. Feeling a little convicted, I went home, poured boiling water into a Pyrex glass bowl, added an herbal tea bag, and put a towel over my head.

Sometimes Ron and I would shop together for groceries and chat. On one occasion, out of the blue, he purchased a fashionable, soft canary yellow, 1940's-style, knee-length belted dress with shoulder pads for me to wear at the office. Though it wasn't exactly my style, I thanked him and wore it a number of times. He certainly did have an eye for clothes.

During a lunch hour at work, Ron and I went for a walk one day and chatted about how he donated blood to the Red Cross blood bank. This was around 1978, before anyone knew about HIV and AIDS transmission. Almost anyone could donate blood no matter what his or her sexual history was. His air of selfless benevolence made me feel stingy because I wasn't donating blood regularly every few months as he did. Had he known his potentially tainted blood could eventually infect innocent people, I wonder how he would have felt. Ignorance may be bliss, but it can also be lethal. I told him I'd hold off on donating blood until I'd finished maturing, and he just looked ahead with a smugly superior air.

Dad and Ron went out cruising some nights together or on their own, and this could lead to heated fights between them. They fought verbally and even physically once in a while, evidenced with bloodshed. Ron might stay away or be banished for a while, but he and Dad always made up. Often during the early evenings, we'd all clean up and go out for a restaurant meal and movie together. Ron, Dad, Mom, and I would walk through some of the shopping areas in the gay village as a foursome. Mom didn't make a fuss about this new relationship, but her behavior was getting weirder.

One afternoon, standing next to the refrigerator in the kitchen, she told me how she had just seen Dad and Ron touching each other between the legs and on the backside. "Like this," she said, suddenly reaching out to stroke her hand between my legs and up to the top of my shorts. I was angry and humiliated. Her description was perfectly adequate. I didn't need a demonstration. It was creepy enough getting that kind of attention from Dad. Would I now have to be on perpetual guard around both of them?

Thomas found sexually explicit pictures of Dad and Ron taped under an old chest of drawers that Dad had given to him. He brought them over to Bryan's apartment and told me I'd better prepare myself to be grossed out. The photos of both men, posing nude with full erections, had been taken in various rooms of our house, probably on a Saturday while Mom and I were out running Dad's errands. At the sight of these pictures, my knees buckled under me, and I fell to the floor and began to sob. "How could he do that?" I asked over and over again. It was one thing intellectually to know this stuff was going on, but it was something much more visceral and upsetting to see these photos. Bryan was stunned by the audacity of my father engaging in this type of behavior—especially with children in the home. In a voice laced with anger he told us how much he hated homosexuality. I'd never seen him so upset before. He had no respect left for my father. He protectively held me as I inconsolably wept into his chest, promising Thomas he'd bring me home later.

I wondered how Mom would react to the pictures. Would she confront Dad with them? Would she finally develop sufficient spine to shut down their sham of a marriage and walk? Or would she just quietly destroy them or hide them and carry on as if nothing had happened? None of the above, as it turned out. When Thomas later showed them to her, she in turn showed them to a few select relatives and friends as proof of what kind of house we were living in. Unfortunately, no one responded in any helpful way.

That summer, Dad instigated another round of photographic fun. He wanted some formal family photographs taken in our backyard to display on his office desk. Who was he kidding? We were his trophy kids that he could show off at work, something to make him look normal and to show to his boy toys, making them think he was attractive, secure, and affectionate. Even though he had no use for us, Dad wanted Mom and me to look our best and bought us lifetime memberships at a Vic Tanny's fitness center in the gay village. He thought we were too fat and needed to trim down. Dad had paid a lot of money for memberships, and I felt guilty if I didn't at least go every once in a while, but I didn't attend often enough to please him.

And here he was using us as a front for one more of his performances, and I could do nothing about it. He controlled the purse strings, and I knew I had to go along with this charade if I wanted to continue living in our "whitened sepulcher" of a home. His unstable moods and threats of violence—implied and stated—kept me docile. I didn't want to risk physical harm to Mom or myself because I didn't follow through on one of his adamant requests. He demanded I act the part, and once again—just like Mom—I went along with the program.

Not having any nice clothes myself, I asked Mom what I should wear. We muttered our disapproval of this whole farce as I angrily slipped on one of her blouses and an oversized navy skirt and went out to the backyard, knowing all this was bogus. I didn't feel like smiling for the camera, but I did it anyway. I had taken care of Mom since I was eight, cleaned and organized the house, cooked meals, done door-to-door sales, and helped with lawn care. I was well practiced at being exploited and keeping my mouth shut. But Dad had promised me if I helped in all these areas, things would be better at this new house. He had uprooted us from our grade-school friends and placed us in a Jewish neighborhood, where we never would be accepted, just because his new beau lived close by. Obviously, it had nothing to do with our best interests—it was all about him. No matter how well I performed, I never could make my father value me for who I was.

After the first roll of photos had been shot, we looked around and realized that Thomas and Scott were nowhere to be found. They weren't going to play "happy family" for anybody, and so Dad had to scrub the rest of the photo operation. My brothers wouldn't be coaxed into taking part in this elaborate lie, and I couldn't help admiring their honesty and courage in just walking away. True, it wasn't as big a risk for them to take off. As boys they'd always enjoyed more freedom and never endured the same level of servitude requirements I had. Just because I was the girl, I got roped into activities that they never did and was exposed to far more grief.

Sometimes I'd meet Mom downtown at Queen's Park where she worked. We'd stroll over to the Eaton Centre for a salad and yogurt before checking out a few shops. We didn't do much shopping really. It was more of an excuse to have a private chat away from the house. Our conversations were mostly about Dad, as I never really talked much about school or boyfriends with her. She often seemed distant, distracted, and depressed, but all the while put on a face of strength in the midst of the chaos her life had become. Mom had been seeing a psychiatrist who helped her sort out some strategies to cope with the billowing pressures that could cause her insulin reactions to spiral out of control. Her job performance was also suffering.

Dad was very controlling, demanding everyone follow his agenda without negotiation. He verbally threatened both of us and even told Mom he would kill her—or have her killed—if she didn't go along with his demands. Mom was never one for putting up visible resistance, and as much as Dad's worsening temper disturbed her, she gave no sign of this to him. She sought to buy time through apparent compliance, fearing that otherwise he would stop paying the bills. On the sly, she began consulting a lawyer to see what was involved in leaving Dad, but she was uneasy sharing any details with me for fear Dad would then coax that information out of me. Deep down, I believe, she still loved Dad and hoped against all experience that he would change.

She didn't mention legal separation until Thomas and I were sixteen, soliciting our opinions on such a move and warning us that it would be a terribly protracted process because of all of Dad's business, financial, and legal advantages. Thomas and I instantly agreed that she should pursue legal separation. But even after that late start, it took an additional three years to work out. At one point, Mom found out her lawyer was haggling deals with Dad's lawyer behind her back, and wracking up fifteen thousand dollars in legal costs all the while. For five long years, we, lamb-like, went along with Dad and whatever he wanted. Generally, the moment we distanced ourselves from him or didn't do what he asked, he would notice and start making things a lot more difficult. The danger of

Dad's physical threats was always there, ready to be unleashed if we didn't do as we were told.

Abandoned as a wife and lover for close to a decade and a half, Mom started looking for intimacy in some pretty strange places. After work, she sometimes went shopping or to the movies with her ditzy friend, Beverly, who habitually dressed in red and encouraged Mom to tart up her appearance with more provocative outfits and brighter tones of nail polish and lipstick. Beverly was forever hugging Mom or holding her hand, and the pair of them often would succumb to little-girl fits of giggling. If not a full-blown lesbian, I'm sure Beverly's door swung both ways. Beverly and Mom went on day trips together to the countryside and beach, and sometimes Mom stayed over at her place. I knew Mom was starved for affection and was a weak personality, easily drawn in to other's whims, and it seemed to me that Beverly's whims were decidedly erotic.

I didn't trust Beverly's influence on Mom one bit. She was also the one who encouraged Mom to try modeling—a field in which she frankly had no hope of advancing. Mom forked over a lot of money for modeling classes; money that could've been more productively invested in other areas of her miserable life. I don't deny that Mom badly needed a dream at this point, some happier goal or situation toward which she could work. But I knew there was no way Mom would ever be comfortable in the catty world of modeling even if she had the right looks. It was embarrassing to see her get fleeced by these shysters, exploiting her desperate gullibility.

I once found lesbian erotica that Dad and Ron had given Mom under her bed. They'd asked her to join them for three-way sexual intercourse, but she wouldn't go along. Just as disturbing to me was the way she allowed Skipper to mount her slippered foot and masturbate. A few times, I found her in her bedroom fondling Skipper's genital member until he climaxed. She believed the poor little mutt needed sexual release from time to time and was happy to oblige him, mopping up his little love spurts with a tissue. Even when I told her this was wrong and that she should stop, she continued. Then I remembered how she would take turns with my brother and me after our baths as babies, placing us on her foot and swinging her leg back and forth. But however strange Mom's behavior might have become, she was never the initiator so much as the reactor, the accommodator. At heart, I always felt that if only she'd married the right kind of husband, she could have been a June Cleaver.

Scott avoided most of the situation at home by almost never being there. Whenever there was the slightest provocation on the home front, he'd flee. He was about five when Dad became more open about his sexuality, and that was when Scott began getting into trouble with other kids. He always would win the daily fights at school and became a bit of a bully. Even though he was practically illiterate into his late teens, Scott was quietly passed along up each grade in the elementary school system. One got the sense that perhaps his teachers kept passing him so they wouldn't have to put up with him anymore. In spite of ongoing complaints about his poor performance, erratic attendance, and delinquent behavior, Scott never received therapy or tutoring to help him learn to cope.

Dad had already taught him by example how to lie and steal, and, being a fundamentally bright kid, Scott picked up those lessons well. By the age of nine, he was spending a lot of time roaming the streets with slightly older, troubled kids, getting into deeper trouble and sometimes not coming home at night, crashing wherever he could find a free bed. We hardly had any family meals together, so I don't know where he was getting his hot suppers. Mom and I would come upon a month's worth of dirtied clothes stuffed behind the wardrobe in the corner of Scott's room. It was really deplorable. He had precious few clothes to wear, sometimes making it through winter without mittens or a decent coat.

The summer after graduating from grade eight, Scott went on a promiscuous tear as if he were desperately trying to assert or prove his heterosexuality. This kid who was so rarely at home and could always find beds somewhere else in which to flop, made a point of bringing his fourteen-year-old girlfriend into our house, where they rather conspicuously locked themselves in Thomas's bedroom and had multiple rounds of very noisy sex. He might as well have posted a large note on Thomas's door: "Hey, Pops—This is just to let you know I have no intention of turning out like you."

I played clarinet in the high school band and made the mistake of inviting Dad to a concert we gave when I was in grade ten. When he showed up, Dad's eyes nearly popped out of his head as he ogled all the good-looking male adolescents in my school. The alto saxophonist in the band was a kid named Barry. Also our school's pole-vaulting champion, he was in excellent physical shape, a fact that did not escape Dad's attention when Barry came round to the house a few weeks later to help me work on a school assignment.

We were talking in the upstairs hallway when Dad came down the attic stairway, wearing only tight underwear and gawking at Barry through the open slats of the stairs.

"Hey, Barry, do you want to come upstairs and have some fun?" Dad asked.

From the attic bedroom above, we heard Ron darkly mumbling something encouraging as well. Dad stood a few feet from Barry with a salacious smile, striking provocative poses as he continued to make lewd remarks about Barry's body and the excitement waiting for him upstairs. He continued baiting Barry with gestures and words, completely ignoring my furious disapproval. At that moment, if he'd been wearing a peacock tail I would have plucked some feathers, tied them around his neck, and strangled him.

"Dad, stop it," I said. "Just stop it. Go back upstairs and leave Barry alone." I came closer to Barry, trying to shield him as the poor kid hesitated awkwardly, not knowing what to say or do. He'd never faced the crude onslaught of this sort of recruitment before and was flustered in his humiliation. A few days later, Dad came into the dining room (thankfully with some pants on) where an elegant meal was spread and snapped a few pictures of Barry and me sitting next to each other. In the pictures, I'm visibly seething with anger as poor Barry smiles sheepishly, not sure what the polite response should be when your friend's Dad proposes a vigorous round of three-way sex.

One Saturday afternoon, coming home from one of our get-out-of-the-house shopping marathons, I put away the groceries and then went down to our rec room. The sofa bed was open with mussed white sheets on the mattress. And, next to the sofa bed, I saw bunched sheets that I opened to reveal shiny, wet streams of ejaculate, KY Jelly, and brown streaks of feces smeared along one side. In one place, it looked as if someone had sat down on the sheets naked while fluid dribbled out of their rectum, leaving rings of brown stain. Horrified and shocked, I called Mom downstairs, hollering, "Mom, come down here. Please come down here. It's really important."

Mom's brow arched upward in alarm as she saw the dirty sheets.

"Mom, I can't believe this," I stammered. "Just look at this mess."

Cringing, she picked up one corner of a sheet and then dropped it in revulsion. "This is just awful. How could he do this in our house and leave this mess?"

"This isn't even his bedroom—it's a family room," I said. "Do you think he wanted us to know?" I asked.

"No," she said with a defeated note of resignation. "He was probably high on drugs."

I'd heard references to drugs before, but the tone in Mom's voice seemed to indicate that their usage was increasing. One school night, Dad had slipped me a sleeping pill so I wouldn't be disturbed by the sound of him and Ron having sex upstairs.

We silently cleaned up and didn't say a word to Dad for fear that I might be kicked out of the house or Dad would stop paying the mortgage. There was also the constant possibility of provoking physical violence if we said the wrong thing or were less than compliant.

I started to crack under the pressure of my increasingly sordid home life and didn't know how I was going to carry on. I longed to get away from it all. In the school washroom one day, I was staring into the mirror when I broke down in tears. A young woman came in and, alarmed at my distress, asked if I was all right. Embarrassed, I told her I was just a little upset. Later in math class while the teacher was assigning homework, the only words I scrawled in my notebook over and over were *Help me*.

That Thanksgiving, I made a critical first break from my toxic home life by going away with Bryan for three days. I didn't plan to go. It just happened. Dad wasn't home. I was up in his attic lust nest looking for something or other, when I suddenly started screaming, sobbing, and banging things around. Dad had just purchased beautiful twin-framed pictures of flowers in glass vases. In an impulsive fit of anger, not really knowing what I was doing or why, I tore them from the wall and smashed them on the floor.

With his feces-smeared sheets, his neglected wife turning weirder by the minute in her loneliness, and his unloved children fatally unequipped to deal with any of the challenges that life was throwing their way, my father, I instinctively and furiously decreed, did not deserve such beauty. This man—who never apprehended beauty beyond the outermost surface of any living thing and would then discard that thing the second its bloom began to fade and replace it with another—simply hadn't earned the consolations of natural beauty that these pictures embodied. And so I destroyed them.

Mom came running upstairs to try to calm me. She took my hands as I bitterly sobbed and warned her not to even try to stop me from going away. As I packed for the trip, she was kinder to me than usual. I think she knew I had entered into a zone where any sort of parental reproach was futile. She knew I had every reason to leave home at this point. The perverse sexuality, the beatings, the shame, the sexual abuse, the critical lectures—by age fourteen, I had endured such pain in this family that I wanted to get away from it all.

Bryan and I went to Niagara Falls for two nights and then off to a football game in Hamilton. We traveled with another couple. A Jewish man in his mid-twenties did the driving and his eighteen-year-old Gentile girlfriend sat next to him in the front seat. Bryan and I sat snugly in the back, saying almost nothing as we watched the passing scenery. We stayed in a nice hotel built around an indoor pool with a whirlpool at one end. After a preliminary swim, the other couple headed off to their room, which had a Jacuzzi in it. We planned to meet for a meal and a walk later.

Our room had two double-sized beds with a few pieces of furniture. The whole place smelled a little of chlorine, but it was wonderful to be away from the clutches of my dysfunctional family. Though I kept my clothes on, I slept with Bryan the first night. We kissed and held each other for a long time, but that was all. The other couple was a little older and more sexually intimate than we were. The girl was reportedly angling for a wedding ring, but her boyfriend was only interested in the sex. I was there for the refuge from my family, and Bryan, bless his heart, was there for me.

The next evening, everything imploded, and I simply could not lift myself off the bed to go out for supper. I was physically and emotionally exhausted from all the chaos at home, and the machinery of my body no longer responded to even the simplest commands. Bryan watched over me through the night, sleeping in the other bed and leaving me to doze like a sack of potatoes for fifteen hours. The next morning, we got in the car and drove to Hamilton. The football game wasn't very exciting for me personally, but Bryan liked it, and it was great to get away even if I did spend most of my time asleep.

When I got home on Monday, Dad was furious that I hadn't been there for Thanksgiving dinner. More to the point, he was beginning to suspect that I was slipping out of his control. He hadn't been around for holidays for years, so why was he so adamant that I missed this one? I doubted very much that there'd been any sort of special dinner, and indeed there hadn't been. I grinned as I tried to picture all of them crowding around the turkey-laden platter and radiating a Norman Rockwell glow; their happiness complete except for the absence of their beloved daughter. By berating me in such a hypocritical way when I got back, he'd only confirmed why I had to go in the first place. Who was Dad to tell me what to do when he was more interested in his boyfriends than me? When he was more interested in *my* boyfriends than me? He didn't care about me. I had to find another way to survive.

Dad's new concern about domestic togetherness quickly passed. Two days later, Mr. Thanksgiving Family Man had utterly changed his tune. He was coming out of the house dressed in obscenely tight pants (his visibly swollen member strategically placed inside one pant leg) topped with an equally tight see-through shirt. I was appalled at his tartish appearance and told him so, but he wouldn't answer when I asked where he was going. He just pushed past and told me not to follow him as he went to the top of the street to be picked up by someone for another night's cruising.

Emotional Incest

By this time, Dad had moved his office to a more central location in downtown Toronto. He was now president and owner of his own executive recruiting service. I worked for him for seven summers and some weekends and holidays throughout my teen years, organizing his files and the thousands of job applications that came in. I didn't mind this at first as it fine-tuned my clerical skills, but eventually I began to feel used. Dad was a tough employer, which taught me how to compliantly serve under authority. I also worked on client files, sometimes doing client searches. This I enjoyed more, as I could use my mind a little bit. By the age of fourteen, he had me filing, answering phones, doing light typing, running errands, and doing the grocery shopping for the office kitchen—all in high heels at Dad's insistence. But he was always impossibly exacting about the quality of my work so that even my best efforts never met his standard of perfection. I had more interaction with Dad in the office than I ever enjoyed or endured at home. But just like our personal relationship, our professional relationship would be violated again and again when he would call me into his office to criticize and lecture me for up to forty-five minutes at a go.

In addition to secretarial duties, my other job was spying. The interviewees never suspected that this modestly dressed girl mooning about the office was the president's daughter, who was watching and reporting their every move. From the moment the clients and applicants came into the warm, professional office space, I was seated behind a high desk taking notes. I assessed their attire, mannerisms, voice, attitude, and overall appearance and watched how they filled out the application forms that would be passed on to the consultants who would interview them. Based on my preview, the applicant could get five minutes or forty-five minutes with a consultant. I felt empowered having this much responsibility to assess people. At times, it outweighed the more mundane work Dad gave me.

Of course, any work environment overseen by Dad had to be riddled with power games. Dad often instructed me to pass on a compliment to an office employee with whom he was displeased so he could then go in and fire them the next month. Dad believed that any sort of praise invariably made employees slack off and become second-rate performers, and it was my task to assist this natural process along. This and my spying service were little extras, but the bulk of my work was straightforward girl Friday-type fare, and I longed for something more challenging. Dad greatly underestimated my intelligence and the value of women in general. Though by grade thirteen I was taking two advanced-level sciences and two math courses, he wouldn't give me more demanding work. Instead, he handed more responsibility to Ron, who handled all the bookkeeping for the Toronto office and assisted Dad in a host of client search duties.

Watching Dad interact with his employees and colleagues, I saw that he appeared to others as very hard working and professional. He didn't come across with any stereotypical gay mannerisms and successfully hid his sexuality at work until I was in my later teens. When he hosted an office party at our house, he didn't loosen up at all, much to the disappointment of some of his employees, who were clearly in the mood to let their hair down and have more fun than Dad would tolerate. Dad took great care to present a façade of happy but sober heterosexuality. Employees who'd worked with him a long time eventually twigged to the dynamic between Dad and Ron, who worked in the office right next door to his. Ron would run errands, make meals, and help me with the grocery shopping—all subordinate, wifely tasks. Dad often locked his office door and took hour-long naps during the afternoons, and all the office staff accommodated this. But eventually, many of the employees couldn't help noticing that Ron was rarely around during those down times either, only reappearing when the lock was released, the blinds were raised, and office life in the presidential suite resumed. Eventually and inevitably, the office staff started to wonder about this arrangement. Few shared their concerns with me for fear it would get back to Dad. They were unfailingly gracious with me and smiled.

Outside of the workplace, however, Dad's hold on reality seemed to be loosening as the voraciousness of his sexual appetite increased. One afternoon, he called me into his office to show me some pictures from his recent trip to New York's nude beach, asking if I'd like to go there with him. Even though I flatly refused, he continued prodding me, and a few days later, he brought up another opportunity. This time, he wanted me to permanently move with him to the gay Mecca of San Francisco, where he could utilize my charms for his own ends. Being around my father, I learned that even gay and bisexual men liked having good-looking women around them. They were used as eye candy to attract more men. Having already used me to attract sexual partners in the local subcultures, he figured he could use me to attract more men in San Francisco.

The plan was that he and I would pack up immediately, walking out on Mom and my brothers and Ron, who'd all be left to fend for themselves in Toronto. I wasn't taking well to his impulsive invitation, and he tried tempting me further with talk about cable cars, a whole new life, and all the great people I'd meet. I didn't want to leave school and my friends even if the thousand practicalities of moving to a new country and finding some way to support ourselves could be worked out. More fundamentally, I didn't trust a word he was saying. Even if we stayed together and he didn't ditch me as soon as it became convenient, I knew I'd end up living downtown with him, seeing the nightlife in the subcultures, and having to do everything he wanted me to do. I knew that even if I had Dad entirely to myself at the other end of the continent, he wouldn't be with me. I wasn't even tempted to go.

When he wasn't plotting to hurl himself into the sexual smorgasbord of the gay districts of major American cities, Dad made do with his old reliables, spicing things up by shifting the locales of their trysts. I nipped downstairs to the basement one cloudy afternoon, moving through the dim hallway and into the recreation room, where I interrupted Dad having sex with Ron. The two of them were stark naked with Dad crouched over Ron from behind, thrusting away. I stood there in paralyzed shock, unable to move as Dad slowly pulled out, carefully picked up his underwear and put them on, and then walked over to the fireplace and leaned his right elbow on the mantel. He didn't look at me or say a word, though he knew I was there. It was almost as if we were pretending that none of this was real and it had all just been a figment of my imagination. When I finally was able to move, I wordlessly turned around and bolted upstairs. Within a few minutes, Dad came up too and told me in a matter-of-fact voice, "Next time you come up or downstairs, announce yourself, so I know you're coming."

Yeah, right, I thought, but said nothing.

In addition to the grossness of watching Dad plunging his penis up Ron's bum, there was also the issue of germs. Once again, Dad and his nonexclusive partner had engaged in unprotected, fluid-generating sex in a room where family members routinely assembled to watch TV. Such behavior put all of his family at risk for, among other things, hepatitis. Fearing we might contract the disease, some family members and I, including Dad's workmates, underwent hepatitis shots as a precaution.

Not too long after this, I was in the upstairs washroom freshening up after a shower when Dad came in to share some important information with me about hygiene. He pulled what looked like an ear syringe out of the cupboard, got undressed, stepped into the bathtub and filled the syringe with warm soapy water that he proceeded to insert and squirt into his rectum. "You should use this to clean yourself out once in a while too," he told me. "Just fill it up with warm soapy water and gently insert it to douche yourself."

Aghast at the thought of sharing any such instrument with my dad, I muttered a few noncommittal words and fled the washroom, not at all planning on adding this ablution to my hygienic regimen. He pestered me twice in the following days to see if I'd given it a go and then thankfully dropped it.

Between Christmas and the New Year, our happy family flew down to Acapulco, Mexico, for another one of our wretched holidays. Here my concerns about the health risks of the gay lifestyle would sharply increase, and I'd also see evidence of Dad's escalating use of drugs. During our taxi ride to the resort, Dad instructed me to yell out the window to likely looking street entrepreneurs, "Do you have any rocks?" Apparently there were a lot of street drugs available in Acapulco, and Dad knew where all the best drug-dealing areas were. At the hotel, we stayed in separate rooms: Thomas and I in one, Dad and Scott in the next, and Mom all alone in another. Our rooms were situated side by side with access to a balcony fridge used for keeping light snacks such as Coke, bottled water, fruit, and avocados. We ate all of our meals in U.S.-style restaurants.

As we were settling in, Dad warned us specifically not to go near the beach or the rocks leading out into the bay, saying the natives used those areas as a washroom. It became apparent that not only had Dad been to this resort before, it had an international reputation as a gay hangout. My brothers and I spent a lot of time by the hotel pool, where we noticed Dad checking the water's cleanliness each morning. He warned us to keep away from the loud parties at poolside most nights because there might be human feces left in the pool. This is what he was checking for each morning. I couldn't imagine what sort of parties these must be where guests wouldn't have the decency to use the washrooms. But sure enough, Dad found fecal matter floating on the water one morning and told us to stay out of the pool until it was cleaned. When the custodian declined to offer him any assistance, Dad personally took on the job of emptying the pool, then got inside and hosed it all down himself. He then turned on the pump to refill the pool but neglected to add any chlorine.

We went on a boat cruise around the bay and to Black Beard's restaurant for supper one night, and saw the divers on the 130-foot cliffs at La Quabrada. After finding out we couldn't go scuba diving, we shopped in the marketplace for silver bracelets and some clothing, wandering into an area where desperately skinny children were begging. I was deeply aware of the contrast between their wretched perspective on the world and mine. The slums of Acapulco seemed so much prettier when we stood on our hotel balcony where their stifling poverty was bathed in the glow of a breathtaking sunset.

It seemed strange at first to be going on one of these excursions without one of Dad's boyfriends coming along. But in addition to racking up spontaneous encounters with total strangers, Dad had in fact planned to meet a particularly wealthy businessman to consummate a real estate deal with a little recreational sex. While he was waiting for a very important morning phone call from this man, the blow dryer and radio were blaring away at full throttle, drowning out the first few rings. When I picked up the phone and bellowed at the man to speak up if he wanted me to hear him, he quickly hung up. The meeting never materialized. Dad was so angry, he made me feel like I'd just ruined the whole trip—which I guess I had—for him.

Dad suddenly stormed out wearing only his bathing suit, heading out to the rocks where he said he didn't want to be followed. We'd seen other men clambering over those rocks in pairs and small groups, which gave us a few clues that he must be cruising out there. We'd seen this pattern many times before: when things didn't go exactly as he planned, Dad would assuage his frustrations with a round of cruising. When he returned, a full three days later, Dad paid off my brothers and me with some money to go visit a few discos on our last night there, while he checked out the downtown core for any stray cruisers with whom he hadn't already hooked up. Mom stayed back in her hotel room, alone.

Back in Toronto, Bryan and I continued to spend a lot of time together, and it got so that I couldn't imagine life without him. In some ways, I was dependent on him to be almost like a father to me, and our relationship was similar in some respects to the controlling relationship with Dad. Bryan told me what to wear, when we would meet, and where we were going; and I basically obeyed out of long-drilled compliance from an early age. Though he honored his pledge to never force sex on me and his presence discouraged others from making those sorts of overtures to me, in many ways I still didn't have my own voice. After school, Bryan was always there. There was no way of avoiding him, even if I wanted to, and sometimes I was pretty sure I did. During the spring and summer, I'd gone along to visit Bryan's grandmother who was dying and found I couldn't cope with the building grief in Bryan's family. This woman had been adored, and when she finally died, I felt I needed some breathing space, finding the family's grief too much to bear.

The week of her death, I went to the pool with Barry, the champion pole-vaulter who'd been hit on by Dad and Ron. I had no romantic intentions, so I didn't see a problem. My relationship with Barry was fraternal. He'd never touched me or expressed romantic or sexual interest in me. Indeed, Thomas told me that Barry was questioning his sexuality, suggesting that perhaps Dad hadn't been hitting on him in a random way but picked up pertinent signals on his "gaydar." Bryan saw Barry and me at the pool and was very jealous, hurt, and angry with me. He assumed the worst and immediately declared our relationship over and done—a decision that was fine with me, though it only lasted a couple of months until we fell back together again. It was cruel to go through this first and temporary break-up with Bryan right when his grandmother had died, but I wasn't ready for the kind of commitment he wanted and knew I didn't really love him. Deep in my heart, I knew I'd used Bryan to meet some unmet needs and was disturbed at how much this reminded me of the way Dad treated others.

When he knew Dad wouldn't be around, Barry began staying overnight at our house on weeknights for a few months. He was there at least partly to get away from his controlling and abusive father. In an arrangement that was similar to what we'd witnessed with Dad and his string of different male housemates, Thomas and Barry started to experiment sexually. Dad knew about this and didn't approve, though he didn't say anything to Thomas at the time. Discussing it with Scott a number of years later, Dad said he didn't want his sons living his precarious lifestyle. Both Thomas and Barry eventually came to desire heterosexual relationships, though I believe Thomas struggled with his sexuality for years.

And then there was Mom, whose life seemed to be sliding into a deepening morass of chaos and pain. Seeking to assuage her awful loneliness, she crawled into my bed one night and tried to hold me, which I didn't handle at all well. I stiffened up and told her in no uncertain terms to leave my bed and bedroom at once, as this was not comfortable for me. She left but was clearly hurt by the incident. I'm afraid I didn't much care. My peace of mind mattered more.

In reaching out for solace in this way, Mom was taking the emotional incest that riddled our lives to a whole new level. Her eyes were always needy, and to look into them was not a comfort for a child. She was looking to me to meet those needs that were not being met by Dad. She shouldn't have spent endless hours with me, cataloguing her woes and telling me what Dad said or did and her reactions to those things. There are some areas of their parents' lives that children instinctually (and healthily) do not want to know about. Learning way too much about things I could never fix, I somehow felt responsible and that I had to help her out of her struggles. Seeking an easy way out with the least emotional investment, I tried to buy her off, spending my babysitting money on surprise gifts for her, though this didn't do a thing to alleviate her suffering.

She was often so exhausted from work and the burden of being virtually a single parent that she just wasn't there for me as a mother. Because my brothers never seemed to be around, she always would interrupt me, calling me down to clean up the dishes, help her with supper, fold laundry or whatever else she had in mind. Because I took more math and science, and was trying to do better at school, there was often more homework to do as well as tests for which to study. She didn't appreciate my need to study, and I came to feel real resentment around her.

Studying one evening for a test the next day, I went into Mom's room shortly after she had come home from work and found her sitting naked on the bed. She seemed dazed and scarcely recognized me. Her eyes were staring, her mouth was dry, and her skin was sweaty from a severe diabetic insulin reaction. Due to the increased stress in our home, these reactions were becoming more frequent—sometimes four a week. She couldn't talk but only mumbled incomprehensible words at me. Though I made an orange juice-sugar combination for her, I couldn't get her to drink it. Suddenly in a fit of anger, she pushed the glass away and became very violent and uncontrollable with her arms thrashing about and her legs kicking. I called our family doctor, my voice frantic. The doctor said he'd be over shortly. By the time I returned to her room, she'd lapsed back into docility and didn't seem to know me. I'd thrown a housecoat around her by the time the doctor arrived and was able to get her to drink the juice before he left. I had to check on her at regular intervals, and though the rest of the night passed without further incident, my concentration for studying was all but shot.

As if Mom didn't have enough difficulties to bear, she now found a lump on her breast and was scheduled for surgery. I was nervous for her, but there was nothing much I could do to allay her fears. She spent many nights pouring out her feelings and crying alone in her room. Dad, of course, never expressed any concern for her through this uncertain time. The biopsy revealed that she had a benign breast tumor, and shortly thereafter she showed me the scars where they had taken the biopsy.

Just how desperately alone Mom was, was driven home to me when her mother died and our family traveled to Belleville to attend the funeral. In the hotel room a couple of hours before the service, Dad lay in a fetal position on the twin bed and Mom crawled over top of him. She was attempting to embrace him but was coldly rebuffed, eventually lying in front of Dad, conforming to the same position. She asked over and over for him to put his arms around her, sobbing in her need for simple, innocent human contact for a few moments to ease her grief.

In a soft but adamant voice, Dad refused her request. "No, Judith. Don't do this. Leave me alone," he said.

He remained behind her and she insisted. "For God's sake, Frank, just put your arms around me, please."

It was too much to ask. Dad's arms remained stiffly at his sides.

No Easy Answers

I hadn't attended church since I was twelve. I was angry with God for all that had gone wrong in my life and for putting me in the care of such a screwed-up family. For more than five years, I was fundamentally unable to trust Him. With my mannish punk rock haircut, I thought that by carrying a masculine armor of cold indifference I would be able to keep everyone at a distance, including God. But it wasn't working. Eventually, I knew I wanted God back in my life—I just didn't know how.

Thomas recently had earned his driver's license and worked out an arrangement with Mom to purchase a used luxury Monte Carlo. From the middle of our Jewish enclave, it was a forty-five-minute drive to the nearest church with any sort of a program for young people. Mom and Thomas wanted to check out Queensway Cathedral in Etobicoke, and I decided to go with them just to see what it was like. We all liked what we saw and began the regular commute a couple of times a week, attending programs and services and hoping to become members there soon. We hadn't been attending very long at all when I realized what I had been missing in my life and impulsively recommitted my life to Jesus Christ.

At an altar call at a Friday night college and careers program, I raised my arms in surrender to Him, asking for His help to make the right choices. My body swayed as I prayed simply and from my heart with tears flowing down my cheeks. No one knew the painful wounds that were in my heart. I couldn't even fathom them all, particularly those relating to my infancy. I had tried talking to the pastor at Queensway a couple of weeks before but couldn't trust him enough to share details about my family situation. On this night, I went over his head, you could say, and took my problems directly to God.

I thought of the grade twelve essay I'd written that year for English class on the Old Testament book of Job. Job was a faithful man who didn't get any easy or immediate answers from God as to why he was made to suffer so much. Instead, God bombarded him with flashing glimpses, as fast and brilliant as bolts of lightning, that illuminated some much larger purpose and plan that was far beyond Job's comprehension.

Well, I wasn't getting any easy answers either. But with that long-neglected remnant of childhood faith that I too held, I was starting to apprehend some possible link between my faith and my suffering. I felt isolated and broken and still had no understanding of my identity in Christ. There was no guarantee of a comfortable road ahead, but that night my future was committed into God's hands. I chose to walk in faith in the midst of suffering, believing God's redemption could impart the strength and patience I needed to survive.

It took about a year and a half to get my life somewhat cleaned up. I gradually absorbed some basic theological pedagogy and slowly worked up the courage to let go of some places I used to go and some people with whom I used to hang. It was a very messy and erratic process, but God knew that. Some people were going to get really hurt as I chose to follow Christ's way, particularly Bryan. I knew we were not meant to be together, as we shared different views about God.

Bryan had been a comfortable leaning post for me. Over time, it had become easy to do sexual things with Bryan without thinking about the consequences or who I was hurting. I noticed that lately I had been feeling more depressed and morally weak whenever Bryan and I were together and that I was engaging in more sexual activities to dull my pain. Thankfully, God is not afraid to enter into the dirty places in our lives and help us get some rooms cleaned up—even if it takes time. Christ gave me the courage to get out of a stranglehold situation that was pulling me down. Not knowing what love really meant, I had been with Bryan for close to four years. Giving my life to Christ didn't mean I wouldn't make any more mistakes or occasionally slip and fall. The big difference was that this time I was following Christ not because of others telling me to but because I wanted to.

One day after taking those first steps, I was blankly staring out my bedroom window when I was flooded with confusion and anger. "Why God?" I asked. "Why did I grow up in this family? I don't understand." I reached for my King James Bible and opened it at random to see if He would give me an answer. My eyes fell on Isaiah 55:7–9. God did not at that point in my life tell me why. Instead, as in His overwhelming non-answer to the entreaties of

Job, God pointed out to me how much higher His thoughts and His ways are than mine.

Isaiah 55:7–9 reads, "Let the wicked forsake his way, and the unrighteous man his thoughts: and let him return unto the Lord, and he will have mercy upon him; and to our God, for he will abundantly pardon. For my thoughts are not your thoughts, neither are your ways my ways, saith the Lord. For as the heavens are higher than the earth, so are my ways higher than your ways, and my thoughts than your thoughts." Verse 11 reads, "So shall my word be that goeth forth out of my mouth: it shall not return unto me void, but it shall accomplish that which I please, and it shall prosper in the thing whereto I sent it."[1]

I was comforted by those words, and I accepted them as His answer for me in faith at that point in my life. A couple of weeks later, I was similarly strengthened by Genesis 12:1 (NIV), which says, "The Lord had said to Abram, 'Leave your country, your people, and your father's household and go to the land I will show you.'"[2]

One morning, as Mom was getting ready for work, I mentioned that verse to her. She said, "Thomas and I both got the same Scripture this past week from the Lord." That God would talk to all three of us from an identical passage of Scripture was a confirmation to me.

I was a little mystified at how Mom could have continuing regard for Scripture while enduring a home situation so at odds with Christian precepts, but I held back from judgment. I realized that anyone looking from outside could say very much the same thing about me. Fitfully she was trying to hang on to her earlier childhood faith but lacked the strength of character to commit to it absolutely. My own situation was not so very different.

I began to realize, at the deepest level, that Dad would never be able to fill this void inside of me. Only God could. Nor did I fully appreciate yet just what this Scripture passage would mean for me personally. It would be a couple more years until I realized that God was to be taken at His Word. Geographical separation from my family—leaving my father's house—was essential for me to develop my own identity as a person, to come to terms with my past, to experience God's healing touch, and to find His purposes for my life.

Mom had been quite right to fear how Dad would take the news that she was seeking a divorce. He received the news via letter, notifying him that she was seeing a lawyer about legal separation proceedings. He didn't want a divorce. He wanted things to continue as they always had been for his whole marriage. I was standing in the kitchen, preparing a bite to eat, when I heard Mom scream, followed by a huge and ominous thud. Dad had thrown her clear across the room. The sound was so appalling that I was afraid to check on her. Instead, I ran out of the house as fast as I could.

At the tiny grocery store at the top of the street, I phoned Bryan's mother, who told me to come over while she called the police and sent them to our house. Later, a cruiser was dispatched for me at Bryan's apartment. Scott was in the back seat sobbing, saying that after I had left, Dad had been chasing Mom with a knife. Back at home, Mom refused to lay charges for fear Dad would do something worse. Later, she went to the doctor, complaining of pain and learned that she had bruises on various parts of her body, including her ribs. When the doctor asked what had caused it, she lied, saying she had fallen down the stairs.

As the days went by, two more incidents occurred when I wasn't at home. Once he pushed her down in the bathtub, and another time he lunged at her again with a knife. She sustained injuries from the bathtub incident, including cracked ribs. According to the doctor, she was fortunate that her lung wasn't pierced by a shard of bone. Again, she was too afraid to tell the doctor what really had happened.

Next, Dad threatened his children. It was understood that he wanted Thomas and me to attend the University of Toronto even though our marks were nowhere near good enough to get into such a prestigious school, and Dad's interest in our scholastic progress hitherto had been minimal. Thomas and I hatched a rather half-baked plot to get into McMaster University instead, situated in the nearby city of Hamilton. Certainly our grades were more suited to McMaster, and if we could get accepted there, we would also enjoy the inestimable bonus of getting out of our home environment. Money, however, was an issue. We didn't have any and knew that Dad was unlikely to put a cent toward any sort of arrangement that took us beyond the range of his day-to-day control.

Undaunted by these discouragements, Thomas and I surreptitiously went down to Hamilton one Friday to check out dormitories and optional residential apartments near McMaster. We got back home in time for Thomas to grab a sandwich and get changed for his evening shift as a waiter at a restaurant. Shortly after, Dad blew in for his weekend residence at home and was loaded for bear about something, seriously ticked off. He called me into the living room where he sat in the striped chair by the bay window where we kept the tropical plants to gather sunlight during the day. "I want to have a talk with you, Dawn," he said in an irate tone, almost looking possessed. "Where have you and Thomas been today?"

How on earth had he caught wind of our little getaway? Were the phones in this house tapped? Figuring he already knew plenty, I saw no point in being vague or offhand and told him precisely where we'd been and what we'd been doing. He took in my words like fuel to a fire that was already blazing. "You are not going to university in Hamilton," he screeched. "And if you and Thomas ever do something like this again, I am going to put you in blood."

I stood, terrified and transfixed, incapable of devising any sort of response to his threat that wouldn't enrage him more. Eventually, somehow, I ducked my eyes from his malevolent gaze and quietly stepped out of the room.

I went to bed that night in agonizing fear—unable to sleep, wanting only to get away but being too scared to make a move. Once I figured everyone was asleep, I crept out of bed and put on my clothes. I knew the polished oak stairs would creak and possibly alert Dad if I tried to make a run for the door downstairs. So I resorted to the hiding place of terrified children everywhere and ducked into the second-floor washroom, pulling the vanity drawer across just under the doorknob to prevent anyone from barging in.

Thomas came home from work shortly after midnight to find me crying and shivering in the shower stall. I let him into the bathroom and told him Dad had threatened our lives. He comforted me for a couple of minutes, and having him with me helped pull me out of the worst of my quivering fear. He called 911, then woke Mom, and we all waited downstairs for the police. When the officer arrived, he went up to the second level and called up to the attic for Dad to come down. Dad didn't come out immediately, but we heard his voice, slurred from the effects of the sleeping pills, say he wasn't coming down. The officer strongly suggested we should then gather our belongings and leave the house. He asked Mom if she was prepared to lay charges and she hemmed and hawed but ultimately decided against it. If she laid charges, Dad would be hauled off to jail for the night, and she knew he would not let that act of betrayal—as he would see it—go unavenged.

In that case, the officer said, there was nothing much he could do but see to it that we were safely escorted off the property. We put through a late-night call to one of Mom's friends who said she could put us up for the night. We gathered our things, including Mom's legal papers concerning the separation, and were driven to our temporary sanctuary by the groggy husband of her friend.

We stayed there for the night, returning on the Saturday when Dad had left to go back to his own apartment. Thomas made sure the coast was clear by making a number of phone calls and checking out the house thoroughly before we went inside. Mom hired a private investigator and bodyguard who kept tabs on Dad and let us know when he was at work, at his downtown residence, or coming to our house. The investigator was with us when Dad returned the following weekend with Ron. He was furious to discover that all the locks had been changed and we wouldn't let him in. Dad came to the back kitchen window where he saw us huddled together in the corner of the dinette area. He screamed profanities and threatened us and called the investigator a thug. The investigator firmly replied in a no-nonsense voice that calmed Dad down for the moment, reaffirming Mom's right to safety and protection. My parents soon worked out some legal arrangement where Dad was allowed to drop by on a few weekends during the summer to gather his belongings. This also ensured that for the time being at least, he'd continue to pay the whopping mortgage payments that Mom never could have managed alone.

It was in our eighteenth summer that both our home and my twin brother started to fall apart. Thomas was heading for a major breakdown. He'd become dangerously withdrawn socially after a girl he really liked had stopped seeing him. Depressed and not sleeping well, he obtained a doctor's prescription for sleeping pills with the result that other than showing up for his shifts at the restaurant, he spent most of his time in bed. When he wasn't sleeping he was in a foul, cantankerous mood, ready to scrap with anybody who got on his wrong side.

He had a major yelling match with Dad one afternoon about what a crummy father he'd been to all of us, more caught up in seedy dalliances with his joy boys than in doing right by his own flesh and blood. Not even one hour later, I was standing in the kitchen looking out the back window when I saw Thomas chasing after Scott with a paring knife. Thomas managed to stab Scott in the leg, and Scott came running in, needing some first aid. Dad came into the kitchen briefly, attending to Scott's leg. Not caring for the way this day was unfolding, Mom and I went over to visit her best friend to get away from both Dad and my squabbling brothers. We'd been there for a good two hours when word came that events at home had spiraled out of control. I was sitting at the piano, sight reading and playing different selections from some songbooks, when Mom was called to the phone.

Beyond consolation, Thomas had angrily run upstairs to his bedroom and closed the door, moving his chest of drawers against the door so no one could open it. He then proceeded to swallow every last sleeping pill he could find. Sensing that things had become way too quiet, Dad checked the bedroom door and found that he couldn't open it. Softly at first and then louder and louder he called to Thomas, who wasn't responding. Dad called 911 for help, requiring the services of a fire and ambulance crew to remove the hinges from the door and then shove aside the chest of drawers. By this time, Thomas had fallen into a dangerously deep, heavily doped sleep. Thomas was rushed to the hospital unconscious. They pumped his stomach, but much of the drug had already been absorbed into his system, and the doctor didn't know if Thomas would make it.

At the hospital, Dad paced back and forth, his face looking haggard and ashen. I hadn't seen him this upset since the Skipper incident in Florida. He'd lost at least two partners to suicide and was terrified Thomas would die too. I wasn't allowed to see Thomas immediately. The doctors had been waiting to see how he would fare. When he finally started to come around, he slipped right back into the depths of his rage about Dad. It was almost as though the drugs acted like truth serum as Thomas bellowed to everyone within hearing that Dad was queer and he hated him. Dad left in a fit, feeling frightened and embarrassed. Here he'd moved mountains to save his kid's life, and this rage and ingratitude were all the thanks he got. The doctors worked to both calm Thomas down and keep him awake until the drugs wore off. A psychiatrist warned us that Thomas's memory could be permanently impaired by the overdose. He was held in the hospital under observation for a few days and then released.

A couple weeks later, Thomas landed a job as a chauffeur at a resort out west and left home. This was another less lethal way he could escape our household situation. We didn't know if he'd ever be back.

It was almost winter when Thomas returned, significantly changed. With his tips he'd made good money chauffeuring. Drawing on his new found confidence, he planned to make enough money to support himself and move out of our house for keeps. With his larger worldview gleaned from his travels, he began networking with influential people. Thomas took ownership of some life goals and set his sights on college. He was going to prove to Dad that he could make it without him.

A few days after Thomas fled the coop, Scott too moved out even though he was only fifteen. This time it was an argument with Mom that precipitated his exodus. He and Mom were shouting at each other about following rules as Scott stomped out the front door. Attempting to stop him, Mom grabbed the string of white beads around his neck and it broke, sending dozens of plastic bits scattering across the gray concrete porch. It seemed a perfect visual analogy for the unraveling of our home. In hot tears, he ran screaming up the street, vowing to never come back. I didn't run after him. What could I do to prevent what was embedded in his heart after years of unmet needs and neglect? He was smart and had a survivor's instinct. Young as he was, I wasn't convinced that the streets posed more of a threat to his development than our toxic home.

I met up with Scott a year or so later and treated him to a hot meal at a restaurant on the main street just up from our house. I attempted to offer him what solace and love I could during the few hours that we were together. I promised that I'd always be there if he needed someone with whom to talk. I later went to visit him at a house where he was staying with a girl who prostituted herself to get extra money. The place was a sty, and he was sleeping on a ragged futon on the floor. He was making some effort to pull his life together. He was still drinking too much, but when drugs became freely available, he at least had the resolve to stay away from the hard stuff. Nor did he hang with the very worst crowd. I felt sorry for his lot. Scott often went without. And all in all, I believe his childhood had been the crummiest, the most neglected, and abbreviated. Thomas and I were three years older and we seemed to have better coping skills. Also, we usually had each other for ongoing fraternal support in a way that Scott had never known.

So Mom and I were alone in the house as that fractious summer drew to a close. We were the only ones who hadn't yet run away, but there were still enough of us for Dad to fight with.

Two days before I started classes at York University, Dad came over with Ron to gather some silver items and other possessions that he felt were his. When he started packing up the white everyday plates and some eating utensils, I snapped. He didn't need that stuff. He and Ron had oodles of dinnerware at the condo. And what did he expect we'd use after the everyday dinnerware was gone? Our laps and our fingers? In my annoyance I called him a "homosexual"—a term Dad did not want to hear—and he was so angry he smacked me on the ear on his way out the door.

Both my parents had been seeing psychiatrists for years. Dad had been seeing a singularly broad-minded shrink who encouraged him to explore every facet of his sexuality and never seemed to demand appropriate behavioral accountability where his children were concerned. I don't think Mom was terribly frank with her psychiatrist either, but he did at least encourage her to try to find help for us. So early that fall, Mom scheduled a one-off meeting with another psychiatrist, a hospital shrink who knew nothing whatsoever about any of us.

Originally, the plan was for Thomas, Scott, and me to meet with the psychiatrist. But when our appointment finally rolled around on the calendar, I was the only kid who hadn't yet bolted the ancestral pile. So I sat on a chair next to Mom in this large group therapy room as this clueless doctor of the mind posed some open-ended questions about my feelings. I had zippo faith in this process and was too angry to respond, knowing this poor man had no clue of the sheer depth of perversity and violence that pervaded my childhood home. It wasn't fair to him that I felt this was a waste of time. I had only come to accommodate Mom and knew there wouldn't be the time or scope in this single, thimble-deep encounter to get at the roots of anything.

After an hour of notating my unhelpful and monosyllabic responses on his legal pad, the therapist summarized the situation as best he could. His verdict was that all our family members should try to come together now and again to see if we couldn't find some way to work out our issues.

I didn't know whether to laugh or cry. Part of me wanted to leap to my feet and shake his hand, exclaiming, "Yes, my good doctor, that's it! If Sigmund Freud could be here today and witness your insightful diagnosis, I tell you he would weep with envy."

Of course, I said no such thing. Of course, our family had no such talk. Of course, I never saw that psychiatrist again.

Next up for a breakdown was Mom. She was driven to it by the tensions and pressures sustained while trying to win her legal separation from Dad. Dad's lawyer and Mom's lawyer seemed to be in some kind of cahoots, making deals that benefited Dad and bought him time while racking up legal bills of $15,000 for her. Dad seemed to be screening our phone conversations. We felt there must be listening devices on our phones and in the house, and even wondered if private detectives might be following us. A few cars with darkened windows would sit across from our house near the top of the street for hours. I was terrified that someone would break in and I often would go downstairs to make double sure the doors were locked and the windows were sealed. Dad sent vile, threatening letters to two of Mom's oldest childhood friends, effectively terminating those relationships. He didn't want her getting any support, emotionally or financially, from anyone and wasn't bothered that his lowest paid consultant was earning $200,000 a year, while the mother of his children could barely survive.

Eventually, Mom became unable to work for a number of months when her insulin reactions became almost daily occurrences. Sometimes I'd go into her bedroom and find her crying while trying to put on her makeup, and often she'd ask me to help her. It was pretty tricky to apply three layers of Estee Lauder shadow to her teary eyelids. Her bed would be left unmade all day. Clothing was scattered about and drawers and closets were a mess unless I tidied them. The slightest effort or errand became too much for her.

One evening, Mom's sister and husband found her walking aimlessly along the main street at the top of our road. She was very fearful for her life, not sure whether to obey Dad's every word or risk the consequences of separating from him. She'd walked out the door that day, planning to run away somewhere far beyond his reach, but after just a few blocks in her practically incoherent state, she had become confused and lost. My aunt and uncle brought her back home, and, alarmed by the condition of both her and our house, over the next few months they regularly dropped by with groceries and basic essentials to fill our empty cupboards. Instead of crackers, cereal, or popcorn to munch on for supper, now, for a change, there was finally some good food to eat.

When Mom started back at part-time work, she soon discovered that her employer was trying to get rid of her, leaving her with a further sense of insecurity. I noticed she slept a lot more than usual when she was home, but eventually she did go back to work full time—about six months after her breakdown. What helped her was that Dad hardly came by the place at all for about a year and a half.

Being with Bryan used to calm me and help me forget my pain, but not anymore. Now, he too was holding me back from the kind of life I wanted to live. Our relationship seemed doomed, yet it was at this seemingly hopeless point that I became more sexually experimental with Bryan, granting him certain physical pleasures but stopping short of intercourse. I may have been trying to numb my emotional pain, but remembering my recent recommitment to Christ, this only made me feel guiltier and weaker. I knew this relationship with Bryan had to end soon, but I was so distracted and deflated by the dismal circumstances of my life that I had difficulty summoning the will to even contemplate change, let alone enact it.

Some kind of break from Bryan would've made it easier to split, but he was always there. We were both enrolled at York University, where I was supposed to be studying math and sciences and Bryan was studying geophysics. Repeatedly and habitually I'd sort of come to in class, give my head a shake, and realize I'd been taking in absolutely nothing of what my professors had been saying. I wanted to get out of the deadening rut my life had become, but I didn't know how. I was hardly eating or sleeping and often felt suicidal but was too afraid to tell anyone. How was I supposed to make a break for some kind of new life when I had no way of supporting myself in the outer world?

About two months into my university education, the warfare between my parents moved into a new phase, and Dad suddenly stopped paying the mortgage, taxes, utilities, and gas bills. With not too heavy a heart—my marks would've been disgraceful anyway—I left university to earn some money to help pay the bills at home. I applied for a seasonal position at Simpson's department store downtown and got the job. There was a week of training on the cash register, and then my job started in the handbag department. I never would have believed the world had need of so many brown and black purses. That autumn, I was able to lay a number of checks on Mom's pillow to help pay the bills.

After receiving my tuition refund from the University, I impulsively bought Mom two long winter coats—a black dressy one and a rust-colored casual one—and bought a cheap gray one for myself that didn't even keep me warm. Apparently, I was developing something of an unhealthy martyr syndrome. I seemed ready to give everything away, including my life. I kept handing over money and gifts—including a $1,000 Mary Kay kit of fragrances, cosmetics, and magazines in the spring of 1982. I didn't know that by then separation money had started coming in from Dad to the tune of $700 per child per month. Mom didn't tell me this, and when I found out, I felt I had been used and deceived. I ran up to her bedroom and wrote *liar* in red lipstick on her dresser mirror.

I was furious that she'd let me spend so much of my money on her after her fiscal crisis had passed. I'd always felt poor living in that expensive house in an upper class neighborhood. The priorities in our lives were so completely backward. We'd dine on popcorn to save money on food yet hire a housekeeper to come in once a week to do the cleaning. Part of my anger was directed toward myself for having the same screwy priorities in spades, squandering money needed for essentials on frills like cosmetics. I was furious at myself for wasting money, time, and opportunities, and for spinning my wheels in such a rubber-burning, smoke-belching frenzy just to stay in the same wretched place.

I broke off my relationship with Bryan at Christmastime that year. It was the healthiest decision I'd made in a long time, but I handled it poorly. I felt horrible and very nervous. I was supposed to meet him early one evening to formalize the break but chickened out. Instead, I gathered all his books, sweatshirts, and other items that had drifted into my possession during our five years together and, with the help of a friend, drove it all over to his family's apartment. I quietly placed all this stuff in neat piles outside his apartment door and slipped away without saying a single word to anyone. That was definitely poor form. But then somebody else took all these items inside and tossed them all over the living room floor. Assuming that I had done this shabby thing, Bryan stuffed all my belongings into garbage bags and dropped them off at the curb of our house. Not knowing why those bags were there or what the contents were, the trash collectors picked up the whole stash on garbage day and carted it off to the dump.

It was a ragged end to what had been, all in all, a real lifesaver of a relationship for me. I needed Bryan's protection, affection, and security as a vulnerable teen. Any other guy would have taken advantage of me. Having Bryan kept the creeps away—the ones who wanted to use me and rip me apart. Though I wasn't very grateful at the end, I am thankful today for Bryan's dogged dedication to me despite my unpredictable moods and poor understanding of love. Bryan accepted me as no other boy had, and my interactions with his family gave me a much-needed glimpse of what a true family could be.

NINE

Tall, Dark, and Handsome

O ne morning that spring when I had the entire house to myself, I was sitting on the steps that led up to the attic. The sunlight was streaming through the hallway's small octagon-shaped window like a warm benediction. Like the heroine of a Jane Austen novel, I was beginning to understand that marriage was the only option for me. It was too expensive to live on my own. I had only a high-school education, and most work paid women low wages. I knew I wouldn't be at home much longer. None of us would. All of our days were numbered in that unloved house full of expensive furniture. We were scattering to the four winds, and it was incumbent upon each of us to do what we could to secure a safe place to land, live, and perchance even to thrive.

I headed out on a short walk to clear my mind. I remembered hearing on a religious TV program how a woman had asked God for a husband and had received one. I'd been skeptical about her story, but I wasn't too proud to give it a try. I did not ask for money or position or comforts. All I required was a decent man who shared my faith and would be willing to share my life. So I prayed, "Lord, give me a husband who is tall, dark, and handsome, who will not have blue or brown eyes but in between. I want him to be a Christian." I was standing in the lane near the top of the street, behind the storefronts with upper rented levels, and in speaking this prayer, I realized with a great rush to my heart that I had meant every word of it.

About three weeks later, I met a gray-eyed, Catholic-raised young man named Vince. We were waiting at a bus stop near Queensway Cathedral and were both on our way to a weekend fasting and prayer retreat with the college and careers group at the church. We ventured upon a light conversation while waiting for the bus to pick us up, and I was struck by Vince's mysterious distance and gentleness and asked a few questions to find out more about him. He was studying at a theological school and had been attending this church for a few years.

When we arrived, the pastor gave a short introductory talk in the chapel area, asking us to find a same-sex partner to pray with afterward. Vince and I sat together, and as everyone else had already paired up, he was my partner. I prayed a general prayer asking for God's will and direction in our lives. I discreetly attempted to look into his neither blue nor brown eyes, trying to take a deeper reading, and wondering why I had met him in this way. I liked him and wanted to get to know him better. Thomas officially introduced us later that evening just before we left for our separate dorms for the night. Vince left a good impression on me, so I looked out for him the rest of the weekend, but we didn't connect. At home while doing the dishes, I mentioned Vince to Mom and told her that I wanted to see him again.

A few weeks later, Thomas was driving to a theological college in Peterborough where he was thinking about taking some courses related to his studies. Mom was going with him, and though I didn't feel the least bit interested, they both insisted I should come along. Possibly, they had ulterior motives. As I sat with Mom in the backseat, leaning up against a pillow because of menstrual cramps, Thomas stopped to pick up another student who'd be providing directions to the college. I vaguely wondered who this boy was but didn't really care until I saw it was Vince. He was just finishing his first year at the college's three-year program for a ministerial diploma and would help us get there and show us around the place. I couldn't really see him from my semi-prone position in the backseat, but I strained to listen to his calming voice as he talked about evolution, creationism, existentialism, and eschatology. We exchanged views on these topics, and he impressed me with his knowledge of the Bible. A few weeks later at the church's college and careers program, Vince came over and handed me about a dozen books to look through, all touching on subjects we'd discussed that day in the car. I was impressed by his detailed memory of our conversation and his thoughtfulness in bringing the books for me to borrow. I read them all and returned them within a few weeks.

Later that spring, Thomas and I attended a play at Queensway Cathedral. Seeing Vince in the crowd, I asked him to sit with us. Over the summer months, we spent more time together after various church services and functions, either heading out to restaurants for endless cups of coffee and conversation or going back to my house. We shared a common faith in God and a desire to learn and grow. Vince had a quietness and stability that really attracted me to him. I liked the fact that he never resorted to sexual innuendoes of any kind in our conversations. Though it wasn't love at first sight, we were fast becoming very good friends, and there seemed to be something significant about the way we kept bumping into one another every time we were at church. It seemed that whenever we prayed, our prayers were answered.

We prayed for peace with God for Vince's father who had become what Catholics call "lapsed" in his practice of the faith. We prayed for provision for Vince's schooling and that doors would open for him in his pastoral internship. One day, I asked God to confirm if Vince was the one for me by having him reach out to hold my hand, and that very same day Vince asked permission to hold my hand. Why were these things happening? I fancied that Vince would some day become a pastor. Was there a possibility that we would come to mean more to each other and that I would be good enough to help him in that work?

I felt that I always needed a boyfriend to provide a measure of protection and security. My mother was similar. Now that she was separated but not divorced—the divorce would take another six years to work out—Mom was using an expensive dating service. I regarded the men friends she brought around as strangers, and I didn't trust them inside the house or my heart. That Christmas, my brothers, Vince, and I went to a nice restaurant to meet Mom's latest boyfriend, a good Christian man whose first wife had recently died. His adolescent children were also there, though we hardly spoke to them or even looked at them during the meal, except to be cordial with our hellos and goodbyes. It was hard in the midst of so many unresolved issues in our own family situation to even consider taking on another father figure, no matter how nice or normal he was. I sensed, too, that this man's children were wary of sharing their father with us. I can see why stepparenting is challenging even in the best of situations. Mom soon broke up with him and continued to check out other men.

Before long, there was another well-to-do man uncomfortably perched in our living room, waiting to meet me. Mom felt he was serious about her and instructed me not to mention anything about Dad or the details of our situation. I really didn't want to have any part in this but put on some nice clothes and went down to say hi. I thought I was prepared to be civil, but as I approached him, I couldn't help but blurt out, "I'm only seeing you because Mother has asked me to. How do you do, sir?"

I couldn't go through with this charade, and, sensing the wall of resentment through which he'd have to hack his way to get closer to my mother, the man presently dropped the courtship, and we never heard from him again. Amazingly, Mom didn't seem all that upset with me. Nor did I feel guilty for ruining this affair. I wasn't about to aid and abet my mother as she deceived yet another man about her health.

Bearing no ill will for the way I had scuppered her romantic prospects, later that summer, the night before Vince was going off to Peterborough for his second year of college, Mom encouraged me to get his address so I could write to him. I raced after Vince as he walked through the church's sanctuary, and tugged on the tails of his jacket. He turned around, surprised, and we stood next to the foyer doors exchanging phone numbers and addresses. I was giddy with a secret hope that something would come of this long-distance relationship with Vince, but I wasn't sure. Would we be just friends? Would we even be that when he heard the whole story about my family?

In our first letters, we shared more about our interests and studies and our desire to live for God. It seemed we were dancing around awakened feelings toward each other, but neither of us wanted to commit quite yet. By the second letter that autumn, we knew we had developed feelings for each other and were openly and honestly sharing from our hearts. Vince and I would see each other every second weekend while he went to school, and otherwise we got to know each other through the mail. In this gradual and measured way, Vince began to vividly express his deepening feelings for me. I had never received these types of letters before from any man. The romance and warmth of his words were a contrast to his usually diffident demeanor. He expressed how his heart ached being away from me, and told me that he wanted to hold me when we were together.

Vince often would come by and pick me up for three or four hours on Friday evening, so we could grab a bite to eat and talk. On Saturdays we would spend as much time as we could together bike riding, checking out book and music stores, visiting with a few church friends, and taking time to share our thoughts. We went for long, rambling walks through my Toronto neighborhood, and I visited him at his school in Peterborough as his girlfriend. His roommate, Karl, was especially interested in Vince's newfound treasure. Karl was a reserved and moral young man whom Vince trusted implicitly.

Knowing that Vince was becoming quite serious about me and feeling it would be dishonest to withhold details about my upbringing until some later date when he was committed to me, I decided it was time to come clean, to drop the big one. I didn't want to drive him away, but neither did I want to repeat the patterns of deceit and secrecy that had rendered my parents' marriage unworkable. I invited him to Gatsby's restaurant in the gay village. For the first hour and a half, I barely touched my dinner as I talked non-stop about Dad's homosexual liaisons. To my astonishment, Vince was not repulsed and expressed no hesitation about having a deepening relationship with me. Learning about my troubles and discerning the mountain of issues I would have to work through didn't make him want to cut and run. He seemed to see and love something in me, and that clearly overcame whatever reservations he might have had about the baggage with which I might have been saddled.

That winter, Vince invited me over for a lunch to meet his father and mother. His father, Alexander, a lawyer from Poland, was raised Russian Orthodox because of his mother's heritage and was now a nonpracticing Catholic. He thought he was a "good enough" Catholic and paid minimal heed to the idea of sin. Alexander had been a prisoner of war in Germany. He was eighty years old and looked it. Vince's much younger mother, Catherina, was a former psychiatric nurse and was staunchly Christian Reformed. I was greatly relieved that this well-educated couple didn't flaunt their learning in any way. There were no airs or snobbery. No attempt to impress or intimidate me. Their identities seemed securely established in their sense of family. Alexander shook my hand and looked deeply at me, thoroughly sizing up this prospective mate for his only child. He threw me a few approving glances as we ate our meal of minced salad, fried steak with onions, and mashed potatoes, all the while asking questions so he could get to know me.

According to Catherina, Alexander immediately liked and approved of me—especially citing what he saw as my integrity and etiquette. If he seemed to be in a hurry to get to know me, he was. Frequently coughing and dousing his irritated throat with shots of brandy, Alexander knew he was dying from a triple whammy of emphysema, bronchitis, and brain cancer and wanted to know there would be grandchildren. Vince's parents' acceptance of me meant a lot and moved our relationship an important step forward. However, this was not an easy time for Vince; he knew his father was not long for this world.

Early the next year, I had taken part-time work with Boot's Drug Store as a cashier. One Friday in February, I was transferred to a store at Bathurst and Lawrence just for the day. That whole day, I had an urgent sense that I must pray for Vince's dad and his relationship with God, having no clue that Vince had just rushed home from Peterborough to be with his dying father. His father, though ill, agreed to pray the sinner's prayer and ask for Jesus to come into his heart. Vince had been praying and fasting for his dad for two years, asking God to send someone else to minister to him. But here it turned out to be Vince who led his father back to a deeper relationship with God, while simultaneously deepening their own father/son pact during their last moments together on earth.

Shortly afterward, Thomas and I got the call that Alexander was dying. Vince picked me up the next morning, and we bought a foam mattress for Alexander. He was feeling every spring in his mattress after the priest had visited him, given him communion, and read him the last rites. Alexander felt dizzy and very nauseated after taking communion and was concerned he may not be in his right mind for long. Indeed, he was spending so much time drifting between sleep and consciousness that hallucinations were becoming very vivid for him. Suspecting the priest might have poisoned him to hasten his death, he asked Catherina to make sure Vince and I were around him that Saturday while he was still reasonably coherent. That afternoon, Alexander called both of us over to his side. He looked at me, took my hand and placed it in Vince's, and then clasped his hands around both of ours. It was a profound moment. He then spoke blessings on our future engagement, our marriage, our children, and our life together. I was deeply moved by both the pathos of the moment and the significance of his pronouncement. That was the last time I saw Alexander.

All day Sunday, he was in and out of consciousness. Very early Monday morning, as death drew nigh, Vince's mom was at his side. Suddenly sensing she should say something, she burst out, "Hallelujah! Hallelujah! Hallelujah!" Alexander's eyes opened and he said, "I see a light." Then he took his last breath. Catherina, knowing he was gone, screamed for Vince. "Pop's gone! Pop's gone!" Vince came down and looked at his father's vacated body as his mother described the whole experience. In her grief she had joy, knowing he was with Jesus. And she marveled at how wonderfully peaceful his death had been.

An ambulance was called and took Alexander to the hospital morgue. Later that morning, Thomas and I went over to support Vince and Catherina. Thomas took charge and at Catherina's request made all of the funeral arrangements for the family. He helped Catherina get four plots at the cemetery and pick out a humble casket for Alexander. With the oxygen machine having run constantly for the last six months to assist Alexander's breathing,

Catherina had not enjoyed a decent night's sleep for a long time. Thomas and I phoned around to make a few more arrangements, and then we took Vince out for breakfast while his mother got a few hours of rest.

Thomas, Vince, and I sat in a pancake house along Eglinton close to Mt. Pleasant. Vince looked shocked and grieved but encouraged that my brother and I were there by his side. In his state of utter distraction, he ordered peppercorn steak on the side— something way too hot for breakfast. We discussed the agenda for the next few days. There were a lot of errands to run and people to call before the visitation and funeral. A funeral at St. Casimir's Roman Catholic Church was planned.

The visitation was quiet with only a few people showing up as I stood by Vince and his mother near the casket. In comparison, the funeral service was vibrantly colorful with many warm Polish friends and neighbors paying their condolences. Vince and a cadre of boyhood chums carried the casket out of the church and into the curtained black hearse. It was a short procession to the cemetery for the burial. A small group of us stood at the opened grave as Catherina wept. "Oh, Pop, I'll miss you," she said. Tears jetted down her cheeks, and I wrapped my right arm around her. She wanted to be with Alexander in heaven. Vince was quiet, taking in the reality of the loss and poking with one foot in the cold, dark earth that had just been dug up. Thomas and I huddled close, listening to the priest pray.

Later that same February evening, Vince's neighbors from a few doors down—older, unmarried twin sisters—invited us all over for deli sandwiches, salads, desserts, and tea served on fine china. It was a beautiful gesture, reaching out to the bereaved in their grief and offering comfort and hospitality. Vince had grown up in a closely knit, working-class, Polish neighborhood with parents who really cared for him. This was a culture that valued and sustained lifelong, sacrificial marriages where children were raised in a community of like-minded people of the Catholic faith. That same cultural grounding was evident in the shops, banks, and businesses of this neighborhood.

Catherina and I became quite close after the death of her husband; she loved to reminisce with me about Alexander's fatherly and husband qualities. Catherina had a memorial for Alexander set up in a corner of the house where his bed used to be. She placed a large framed picture on the wall and a sentimental poem just below. She'd stand before this makeshift shrine for minutes at a stretch, telling stories about their life together and pausing to wipe tears from her eyes as she looked upon her beloved. I discovered that Catherina, in her grief and fatigue, was neglecting to eat properly and had become quite dangerously run down. When she developed an infection, I thought it would be best if she were placed in some sort of attentive care until she got back to her old form. She never forgot my kindness in arranging for a brief hospitalization. She was always grateful to me for loving her at a vulnerable time when she otherwise might have allowed herself to die.

Vince's loss only deepened our relationship, which seemed a good sign. Rather than running as I had when Bryan's grandmother had died, I drew closer to Vince. We began a series of progressive commitments to one another, having received the support of both of his parents. I had been afraid of commitment, marriage, and having children. So these much slower stages of commitment were easier for me. I was drawn to Vince's quiet honesty about his feelings, his uncluttered simplicity of lifestyle, his strong sense of morality, and his gratitude for life's gifts. When I was with him, he told me what he thought and felt, never putting on airs and never trying to be anyone but himself. He never lied to me or took advantage of me sexually or any other way. I knew him to be a man of integrity. After so many years of restless disquiet, Vince provided me with a deep sense of rest in my soul. In the easy mental climate of his presence, I found I could read books, retain information, and study more successfully than I ever had before.

That summer, Thomas, Vince, and I attended a family reunion on my father's side. It was one of those rare times when Dad actually showed up to see his family—though his reasons for doing so had more to do with showing off than being with relatives. He came in after everything had started, wearing an expensive sporty black suit, and all eyes were on him. He loved the attention, showing off how successful he was. When I went over and asked if he'd like to meet Vince, he totally snubbed me, pretending I didn't exist. I rushed into the kitchen, where I burst into tears while Vince stood next to me, rubbing my back. I was both cut to the core and pig-biting mad. The coldhearted gall of the man! A few moments later, Thomas, Vince, and I headed out en masse, not caring one bit if our exit made him feel a little uncomfortable or left him with something to try to explain to the other guests.

When Dad finally consented to meet my boyfriend, it was just after Vince had finished working two consecutive shifts and had been up for about thirty-six hours. Dad had boorishly declined his opportunity to meet Vince when he was better rested and suited up and demanded instead that Vince come to his office for a get-acquainted chat just after five in the afternoon. Vince came in wearing work clothes from his factory job, guaranteeing that for someone as sartorially punctilious as Dad, that all-important first impression would be less than favorable.

Vince clumped through to Dad's inner office in his steel-toed shoes, shook hands, and sat down, looking around as they exchanged small talk and taking in everything. By the time I slipped in to join them, Dad was into one of his anti-homosexual harangues, saying he didn't like their characters or their personalities and he would never hire one. As if Dad was something other than a practicing homosexual and his homosexual partner wasn't on the payroll and working right next door? It was pitiful in a way. Did Dad think I wouldn't mention a little matter like his life and home-wrecking gayness to the man I hoped to marry someday? That it would remain our little secret?

Vince failed his audition. Dad said Vince was too poor, and saddled with him I never would have nice things. Having worked hard to overcome his own poverty and make a better life for himself, Dad didn't want to see me going backward financially. Vince would never be able to take care of me properly, Dad said—seeming to imply that he had. Dad couldn't see that what I wanted first of all was a moral man. Too many men I knew with money flaunted it and were faithless womanizers, easily discarding their wives for younger women. Yes, my thinking was a bit twisted perhaps, seeing all rich men in a negative light—but this is what I had seen growing up, and there was no way I was going to live through the pain of unfaithfulness as my mother had.

Though Vince would never behave disrespectfully to Dad, he wasn't very impressed with him either. Vince's perspective was that

Dad wasn't trustworthy and had precious little depth of character, valuing everybody by their apparent financial success.

That fall, I enrolled in a part-time program at the University of Toronto, studying psychology, biology, and sociology. Vince badly wanted to take his third and final year at theological college but didn't have enough money for all his courses and his residency. At just about the last possible moment, a letter came from Germany, announcing that some monies were owed to Alexander's estate, accruing from the term he had served as a World War II prisoner of war. The amount precisely matched what was needed to cover Vince's school costs.

Vince and I attempted to balance studying and exams with seeing each other. Most of the time, Vince was an enormous comfort to me. However, there were times when I'd suddenly fall prey to an instinctive fear of a deeper commitment and even thought about breaking up. Vince called me one Friday to let me know he was back in town and wanted to meet. I hesitated, saying, "Vince, something's come up. Maybe I'll call you later this weekend." My vague excuse about why I couldn't see him struck him as odd.

Sensing my fear, Vince called back a few minutes later and asked, "Dawn, what's going on?"

"I feel like I'm on a train that's moving too fast, and I can't stay on it," I told him. "I'm really afraid of where our relationship is going. Do you understand what I'm feeling?"

Vince didn't panic but calmly let me think this through. I knew if I stayed on, marriage was likely, and I was frightened. While I loved Vince and knew that marrying him would be my surest ticket out of my sick and disintegrating home life, I hadn't really considered marriage seriously and all that it would bring. The possibility of having children wasn't even on the radar at this point in my life. I had no desire for children. My own childhood had clinched that. Not only was I unsure about commitment, I didn't know what would become of me if I went where Vince was going—likely away from Toronto, where I'd lived all my life. Vince was already beginning a ministerial internship in Strathroy, working with a senior pastor before graduating from college in the spring. A pastoral position could place us anywhere, and I wasn't sure I was ready to take such an open-ended step. This was my chance to hightail it out of my home situation and get away from the controlling influence of my father. Tempting as that was, I knew any move I made had to be God's will.

"Vince, this is a huge decision, and I don't want to mislead you," I said. "You've been really good to me, and I don't want to hurt you."

I also had a lot of uneasiness about possibly becoming a pastor's wife. I hadn't exactly grown up in a strait-laced home—something I assumed was an essential prerequisite for anyone considering such a station.

Vince quietly listened to my concerns. Rather than pressuring me, he made a suggestion. "Dawn, you should fast and pray to see what to do. Give it a week, and then you can tell me your decision." And with that, we hung up.

I attempted to fast and pray, but it just didn't work no matter how hard I tried. I was terrified at the prospect of handing over my entire life to just one man. And I was just as terrified that I was about to throw away the only man I'd ever known for whom was worthy of taking that kind of risk. Could I trust Vince with my life? Was being with Vince God's will?

A week later, I called Vince, and he came right over. He couldn't say much in the way of preliminaries as he waited to hear my decision. When I told him I hadn't been able to fast or pray and my stomach had been in a perpetual knot, he asked if I loved him.

"Yes," I told him. "But I'm afraid."

He placed his hands on my shoulders and looked at me as I laid out the sort of doubts with which I was struggling. I told him how I'd never seen a shred of continuity in my dad's relationships and how difficult I had found it to stay with any one person for long. I was trying to overcome my deepest fear—abandonment—by heading it off at the pass. I was thinking about dropping Vince before he could drop me. Could I trust Vince to always be there for me? As I shared these feelings and thoughts, Vince exhibited constancy and desire for God's will. He wasn't pressuring me to stay with him. Had he, I'd have run.

I had to consider that when I was with him, I felt a pervading sense that everything would work out no matter what the circumstances. Vince had this enormous, solid faith in God that gave me a sense of security. The "soul rest" around Vince was inestimable. In some ways, looking back, he seemed almost angelic—not the sort of guy I'd usually attracted before. He didn't hit on me, gawk at other women, physically or verbally assault me, swear, lie, or cheat. When he said he'd be at my house by a certain time, he kept his word every time. He was the truest man I'd ever known. That day I wavered for the last time. I chose to continue our relationship.

Of course, the next logical step was to become formally engaged. On some abstract level I knew this, but I was a little slow to realize that that was where we were, that now was the time to cross that threshold. Vince took me to a jewelry store in the Eaton's Centre.

Even when he asked which set of rings I preferred, I didn't twig to the fact that he was thinking of buying them for me.

A few weeks later, after a wonderful meal at a dimly lit restaurant, Vince took me outside to the patio. It was chilly, and Vince took off his jacket and set it over my shoulders. There were mythological statuary and a ring of stone benches around the perimeter. A little corny perhaps, but in the dark night air with the teeming city all around us, these ghostly satyrs, fauns, and nymphs were the witnesses of Vince's wooing of this young woman who was so frightened of commitment. Had she but known it, Cynthia Dawn was standing at a major crossroads in her life. All of a sudden, Vince was kneeling at his crossroads. He dropped down onto one knee, held forth a small, brown, felt-covered box and asked, "Dawn, will you marry me?"

Without hesitation, I flung my arms around him and said, "Yes." We kissed and held each other, and then he helped place an engagement ring on the appropriate finger of my left hand. Splaying my fingers and slowly turning my wrist so the diamond caught and reflected the evening's light, only then did I recognize it as one of the rings we'd looked at a few weeks before.

I later found out that Vince had taken most of his coin collection that he'd inherited from his father and sold it to buy my rings. Hearing this, I couldn't help crying. No one had ever made such a sacrificial gesture for me before. Though my father had far more materially, he'd only purchased fake or cheap jewelry for me. Here Vince, a cash-strapped theology student, was giving up a sentimental inheritance from his father for me. What made Vince's sacrifice even more significant was his father's deathbed blessing of our marriage, children, and family life. And now the rings that his bequest of rare coins had bought were the ceremonial sign that the union he had so desired for us would become a reality.

Wedding Plans

I often thought that I would ride the stars to find a way out of my household and, now, appropriately enough, Vince drove me back to my house in his battered green Nova. I ran upstairs to wake Mom and tell her the news. She didn't take it well. Perhaps I should've waited until morning. She was shocked, she said. Too shocked to tell me how she felt about it until the following day. That gave me advance warning that she was less than delighted.

The next morning, she came into my bedroom and told me she'd always said she wanted me to marry a wealthy man.

Exasperated, I turned on her and said, "Mom, I love him. And you like him too. You're the one who told me to grab Vince and make sure I got his address and phone number before he went back to college."

Then I remembered how Mom had slipped a pamphlet under my bedroom door a few years earlier when I'd gone on a few dates with a Jewish boy, explaining why I should never be "unequally yoked" in matrimony. "Mom, you're the one who encouraged us as

Christians to go out together," I reminded her. "You even accommodated Vince in our home. Why the about face?"

She didn't have a ready answer for that and retreated to her room to get herself ready for work.

When Dad found out, he was angry too. I visited him at his office, and he called me closer to look at the engagement ring. He told me, "You should have come to me first. I could have obtained a larger diamond for the same price Vince paid." Dad didn't realize I was looking for something a lot deeper than materialism in a man. I was fed up with smooth-talking, good-looking, unstable men who were not content for long with their job, home, car, or partner—always looking for something better about which to brag. Such fickleness wasn't limited to gay men. I saw these heterosexual butterfly boys every day in Dad's office. When I was around the young men in our neighborhood, I saw their nice cars and the way they used Gentile women and later discarded them. Enrolled once again at university, I noticed that no matter whether they were professors, tutorial assistants, or fellow students, different men continued to hit on me and sexually harass me, making it awfully difficult to study well. It was next to impossible to get help from the support network that was there to supposedly help women. If I lodged a complaint, I knew the man wouldn't be disciplined, and if he was one of my teachers, I could face low marks, failure, or worse. There was no sanctuary anywhere. The workplace, the suburbs, the cloistered walls of academia—they were all rife with the heterosexual version of the same sort of aggressive libertinism that ruled and ruined my father's life. There was no way I was going to repeat his mistakes.

While Dad made sure his boyfriend had a good-paying job at his firm, he hadn't offered any significant opportunities to any of his children. Thomas desperately wanted to prove himself, so knowing how much it would get up Dad's nose, he took a brief holiday from his regular work and snagged a consulting job at a big Toronto executive recruiting company on the waterfront. Thomas was so astonishingly successful that he quickly became the top commissioned consultant there, much to Dad's outrage and fury. My twin was so good at racking up huge commissions that he was in direct competition with Dad and trounced him on a number of deals. It was a bit jarring how he went about it, but I understood how important it was for Thomas to prove himself and win the sort of accolades from his boss that none of us ever received from Dad.

That December, I'd become ill with stress while tending to Mom's neediness, so I temporarily moved out to get a break and do some serious studying for a major psychology exam. I was cramming over at Catherina's house while Vince was away in Peterborough, and that was where I received the call from Thomas. He told me Mom had come home from work in an insulin reaction and had run into serious trouble. There was fresh snow on the ground and it was dark by late afternoon. She was making her way down our street when she had become confused, fell to her knees, and couldn't pull herself up, so she had started crawling to our door. She couldn't focus sufficiently to find the house key in her purse, so she had crawled back down our driveway and across the street to a neighbor's house.

The skin on her hands and knees was ripped open by the dirty salt mixed in with the slush on the road. She'd smeared her cracked and bloodied hands along the front and sides of the beautiful winter coat I'd purchased a year earlier for her. Then, she had collapsed in the snow. A neighbor came out of her house and assisted her until an ambulance came. Mom was kept overnight at the hospital on intravenous to bring her around. Thomas and I felt horrible that neither of us had been there for her. At the same time, I don't know if I could have borne coming upon her in her distress, prostrate and bloody, like some animal that's been hit by a car and crawled away to die.

While finishing off his last year of college, Vince began some work in a church in St. Thomas. He'd already moved from Toronto and was setting up things for us in this small community south of London. I'd come down for weekends and stay with parishioners at the church. Vince preached a few services as I nervously looked on. These people had a different set of priorities than what I was used to in the big city. For the most part, they seemed content with their lot and worked hard to provide for their children. A kind-hearted older woman who was a nurse took me under her wing. Her husband worked for the railroad and they had three beauti-fully behaved teenaged boys in the house. She would set aside the guestroom whenever I came down and made me feel like it was my home. Some of the diaconate families would have Vince and me over for supper, sharing tender details of their life stories with us. I was impressed with how open and trusting people are prepared to be with ministers—or ministers-in-training.

The lives of these families were so radically different from anything I'd ever known. Learning that Vince and I were engaged, the teenaged daughter of one of these families smiled excitedly and took me to her bedroom because she wanted to show me her bridal chest. She didn't even have a boyfriend yet, and here this fourteen-year-old girl had all these beautiful items stashed away that she proudly, carefully, lovingly pulled out to show me: a set of exquisitely genteel china teacups, some handmade doilies and a lace tablecloth that had been passed down through generations along her mother's line, and a bounty of other elegant items any girl would love. I acted like all this was just grand—and it was—but inside I felt like weeping. How I envied this girl and her wholesome upbringing. It never would have occurred to my parents to put away a special chest of items for my wedding day. As far as my family was concerned, my upcoming wedding was some freakish little project of my own that had nothing to do with them.

Vince and I had planned our wedding and reception for the late summer. Dad told me he wanted nothing to do with it, so we had invitations printed without my father's name on them. Vince and I also booked a suburban banquet hall with a deposit of three hundred dollars for a modest reception.

Then, realizing the wedding would go ahead whether he approved or not, Dad made an about face and called me in to talk. There was no way his daughter was going to get married in an inferior manner, especially in front of his relatives. He told me he wanted to pay for the reception, and it was going to be held downtown on Church Street at the Loews Westbury Hotel. He originally wanted the pictures taken at Allen Gardens, right next to the gay village, but thankfully there were no spaces available for the day of our wedding. He was taking control of particular aspects of my wedding, and for this I was both grateful and wary. I talked to Mom about my reservations, and she basically said, "Dawn, this is your father. He has to be included on this day. Just let him do what he wants."

Vince and I discussed the changes to our plans and quickly had new invitations made and sent them out. There was no way we were going to argue about this. We couldn't afford this ourselves and were thankful for my father's intervention. Dad was not going to be outdone by anyone. His brother had just splurged on a lavish wedding for one of his daughters. So Dad was going to up the ante and throw a bigger wedding than anyone else in his family could afford.

A couple weeks before the wedding, Dad called me into the living room because he had something very important to discuss with me. "Has Vince been circumcised?" he asked. And yes, that was all that was on his mind as his only daughter prepared to wed. The entire discussion centered on diseases carried by uncircumcised men and how important it was for men to keep themselves clean. After sitting through these kinds of conversations for two whole decades, my capacity for being outraged or taking offense had dissipated. Well, of course sexual hygiene would be a big deal for Dad. Considering all the men with whom he'd had encounters, he should have been concerned about disease.

"Vince is a virgin," I informed him, speaking slowly, since I knew such concepts would be quite foreign to him. "So it doesn't matter whether he's circumcised or not. He has no diseases. He's never been with anyone sexually."

I rather would have heard Dad wishing all the best for my wedding, or giving me support during this time, or wondering about when we would have children, or what our plans were for settling into a place together. But no. His concerns were strictly limited to the groin, as usual.

I continued working for Dad during our last summer together, making wedding plans during lunch hours and after work. Dad called me in about a week before the wedding and said Ron was very hurt that I hadn't invited him.

"I assumed he wouldn't want to come," I replied. In all the years Ron and I had known each other, I'd put him down as pretty well indifferent where Dad's children were concerned. Apparently, I was mistaken. I stepped into Ron's office and told him I was very sorry for the oversight, and he accepted my apology. The following day, I personally gave him an invitation.

At our wedding rehearsal, I overhead Dad saying to the pastor, "She's too young to be getting married." I recalled that Dad was only twenty when he married Mom. He had no inkling that just like him when he was my age, I was desperate to get out of my environment and make a new beginning for myself. Dropping me off at home, Dad leaned close and confidentially asked if I had any lip makeup he could use. He had sores around his mouth about which he was embarrassed. Of course, I wondered if this could be the early onset of AIDS, which was much in the news at the time. I knew Dad already had a small collection of makeup, including top-of-the-line foundation and a cleansing system for sensitive skin. He needed something more heavy duty than that to cover up those sores. I chose my best Mary Kay lip palette of six colors with lip brushes and gave it to him, not anticipating its return.

There was supposed to be a small reception at our home after the rehearsal, but when we got there, Thomas found Mom outside in the backyard digging holes in a trance-like state. She was having another severe insulin reaction. It had been her intention to plant a long row of pretty annuals in the back garden for the photographer to take pictures the next day. Unknown to Mom, the plan was that pictures would be taken on the front lawn rather than the back. Thomas quickly attended to her with sugar water and cleaned her up. Then he brought out some store-prepared sandwiches and desserts, while our college and careers' friends kindly and understandingly cleaned up the place for the following day. I excused myself to freshen up and go to bed.

It's not unheard of for twins to feel abandoned and even threatened when their closest sibling marries. Something like this may have been going on with Thomas. My twin used to say he wanted to be married on the same day I was, but here I was beating him to the altar just like I'd beaten him onto the delivery table. Perhaps that rankled. My prenuptial sleep started well until Thomas wandered into my room at about two in the morning with a friend I'd never met before and rudely demanded that I get out of my bed. My bridal dress and veil were hanging there, but Thomas demanded I vacate the room so his friend could sleep in my bed. Thomas was so adamant about this, I caved in and slept in Thomas's bedroom, maybe getting four hours sleep. I'm pretty sure both of them were drunk. I was justifiably angry, but told myself to let it go. This was the last night I would ever sleep in this house, and I wasn't about to fight for my right to my own bed. This friend, whom we never saw again, also came to my wedding the next day and sat on the side of the center aisle. He never spoke a word to me all day—though he managed to thoroughly stuff his face at my reception. Perhaps Thomas felt the need to have someone in his special corner as his twin prepared to move out from under into the world without him.

I was thrilled to be getting married. While I hadn't grown up dreaming of this day, and had been pretty obtuse about the niceties of getting engaged, I snapped into gear (perhaps even into overdrive) as the big day approached. I had planned meticulously every aspect of the wedding, packing four pieces of luggage complete with itemized lists for my honeymoon, laying out everything in the precise order that we would need it. My father, my brothers, and Vince decorated Dad's black Cadillac the morning of our wedding, while the five bridesmaids and I dressed for our first set of pictures in the living room.

Perfectly timed, Dad pulled his Cadillac into our driveway while the bridesmaids, matron of honor, and I said a small prayer for the day while holding hands. As I said goodbye to my friends and stepped into the car, Dad gingerly positioned my long white gown away from the door and closed it. We drove to the church and waited at the back door of the sanctuary. In the church awaiting our cue to move up the aisle, I finally had an opportunity to really appraise my father. He was smartly dressed in an ivory jacket and dark pants. His saddened face was smoothed over with the skin-tone makeup he'd carefully applied to add a little color. I could see tiredness in his eyes, as if he were trying to mask some illness. He gently took my hand, and we walked down the aisle. He kissed my cheek as I was given away to Vince and then went to sit next to Mom, making a fine impression for family and friends in attendance. Ron sat a few pews behind Dad. Vince's roommate, Karl, was best man, standing on the platform just behind us, hoping for the day he too would get married.

Throughout the ceremony at The Stone Church, during the afternoon photo sessions, and at the reception at the hotel, I felt both the beauty and sadness of the occasion. Just beneath the outer show of extravagance, the whole day was filled for me with a sense of my parents' regret that I was marrying Vince. Just before the reception, Dad pulled Mom and me aside to some doors that led down a flight of stairs to a small courtyard. We walked together there to gain a few moments of privacy away from the guests. Mom was to my right and Dad was to my left. There was a sinking feeling inside that we didn't need to verbalize. I easily could have burst into tears if I had let myself dwell on the thought of how very little my parents still shared. We had drifted far apart years ago. This ceremony only formalized the unbridgeable chasms that separated us all. For two decades, we had not been there for each other as husband and wife or parent and child should be. Small surprise then that on this special day that calls for grand declarations and vows, we had nothing to say to each other.

Dad had always pushed me to grow up very quickly, to be responsible, mature, and independent so he wouldn't have to take care of me. But at the same time and in another way, he wanted me to remain at age thirteen forever—just starting adolescence and never growing up. Now that I was getting married and moving away, he couldn't quite believe it was happening. He couldn't accept that I was leaving and he was never going to see me much again.

No major debacle happened on this special day. The only hitch was when Thomas, still in doofus mode, took an hour and a half to deliver the wedding gifts back to the house and bring my luggage to the hotel, including my going away outfit. When I finally went down in my pink chiffon dress to say goodbye to the guests, I was confronted with a sight that put the whole day into a sort of twisted perspective. Vince and I originally had planned an alcohol-free reception. When Dad shanghaied our wedding plans, that, along with much else, changed. Coming down the stairs, I saw three of

Dad's reprobate brothers carting off whole cases of Johnnie Walker, Captain Morgan, and Mumm's to their trunks. Some relatives were so smashed, they no longer could stand up. It would cost Dad over five thousand dollars to foot the bill for liquor, beer, and wine—something he would later regret, deciding an open bar had not been such a great idea.

Camp Meeting

We honeymooned for two weeks in Florida, staying at my uncle's condominium. On our own together at last, not once did Vince or I think to plug in the phone, so we didn't know Dad was calling us every day to see if we were all right. On our return to Canada, we said hello to Mom, picked up the gifts, and began our married life together in an apartment in St. Thomas.

By the fall, Dad was pressuring me to come back to Toronto to help Mom move, but Vince would have no part in that. He wisely wanted me to operate outside my father's orbit for a while and work with him on the ministry in our new community. Vince also needed some separation from his mom, because he was feeling her suffocating neediness with the loss of his father. He could not be a husband to her. Catherina knew Vince needed to build his own life, and she, thankfully, gave him that opportunity. Leaving my family situation and moving to a brand-new city with no family members or friends close by was a huge step for me. Dad's incessant phone calls and a sense of unease about the church where we were working made me feel sick with nervousness and worry. It was one thing to physically move out of my father's world, but I began to apprehend that spiritually and emotionally the break would not be so easily made.

We knew something was not right in St. Thomas, and Vince sensed that he might not have the job for long at this church. The senior pastor was secretly planning on leaving the church and needed us there to help as he moved his family along to his next pastorate. Vince and I were disappointed by this turn of events and got a taste of the insecurities of ministry life right from the start. Whom could we really count on? Only God and—please, God—each other.

In our new life together, Vince and I began each day by reading a few passages of Scripture and praying together that God would open doors and provide for our needs. We reminded each other of the many times our prayers had been answered and held tight to our Christian faith. Much of our savings had covered the significant costs of getting married and relocating to St. Thomas. The small pastorate salary did not cover our daily living expenses, so we often cut corners, eating peanut butter, canned tuna, and ground beef as our main protein sources.

Our first Christmas together was simple and warm. We decorated an artificial tree in the living room and placed a few gifts under it for ourselves. We did not have extra money that year to buy presents for others. Though we were living what might seem to others an impoverished life, it felt strangely liberating, even luxurious in a way, to have so few things just between us and feel so enormously grateful. I decorated a chocolate Yule log and created some other treats as we made plans to attend a special church service and visit family in Toronto the following week.

We saw Vince's mom in Brampton on Christmas Eve, sleeping on her pullout sofa bed in a corner of her one-room apartment, where she'd installed a curtain for privacy. This was a major adjustment for Catherina, who had just moved from her spacious four-level duplex home, blocks from High Park, having received below market value for the property. She no longer could walk up the stairs, maintain the house, or afford the necessary upgrades to the dilapidated electrical and plumbing systems, furnace, and roof.

We made a short visit to Mom's luxurious apartment at the Sutton Place Hotel in Toronto on Christmas Day. Dad was there with a large gift for us: a humidifier. Not understanding our situation, he was expecting a gift from us, but we had nothing. He was so hurt he turned away in tears and walked out of the room. I was thunderstruck. This was the first time I ever had driven my father to tears. It seemed my separation from him was causing a shift in our relationship—enough so that he was becoming more vulnerable toward me and expressing his grief. His sudden expression of pain pierced my heart but also gladdened me in a way. He seemed to be longing for the family life he never really had appreciated before, though now it was too late to recapture it. I wished that I had brought some kind of gift for him, though I knew it wouldn't have taken away his regrets of everything he'd missed in years past.

Scott was nowhere to be seen that Christmas, which only magnified how alone Dad must have felt. Ron had gone away to visit his family with gifts in tow. Mom was about to become his ex-wife and retained no special fondness for him. Dad was just beginning to see how very cut off he was from everyone.

Vince and I arrived home late Christmas night. After a good night's sleep, we opened our gifts to each other on Boxing Day morning. We were relieved to be back in our own space, just the two of us. Vince had picked out a beautiful card with poetic descriptions of what was in his heart for me. We listened to Christmas music while unwrapping winter hiking boots for both of us, leather gloves and a scarf for Vince, a bottle of perfume for me, and some small gifts from Catherina. I set our table with a white floral tablecloth, silver candelabra, my grandfather's silverware, and my father's Wedgwood china—all precious wedding gifts. We ate a small stuffed turkey alongside green leaf salad, carrots, and potatoes and gravy, and drank grape juice and ginger ale punch. We shared some extra slices of the homemade Yule log and afterward read aloud the gospel account of the Christmas story. After dinner, we took an extra-long, blister-inducing walk in our new hiking boots and dreamed of what our future would be like together. There was a sense of God's peace despite our imminent departure from this church and the knowledge that Vince ultimately might have to seek work unrelated to ministry. We had each other and the better part of our lives stretching out before us. This was more than enough.

We were home for the New Year, making plans for Vince to find other church work that January, while I aimed to get working on some college business courses, subsidized by the government, and start driver's education. Though things were financially tight, we made it through. A few checks had arrived in the mail the same week, exactly meeting my enrollment fee for the driver's education course—one from Catherina and the other from Dad.

By the next fall, I'd finished my college courses, Vince had found a job fixing typewriters and business equipment in London, and I had landed a job there too at a commercial and residential construction and property management company. We scratched together enough for the first and last month's rent and found an apartment in London we liked and moved in.

After another year and a half, working flat out and picking up overtime and weekend work as well, we were able to move into our own condominium townhouse, which we purchased in late 1986. Catherina came to live with us that December, staying for a few years before moving into her own apartment. Vince enrolled in a number of part-time university courses, working toward a bachelor of arts in gerontology and sociology, and then a two-year diploma in addiction studies through McMaster University. I began studying to be a Certified Management Accountant, taking the very same course Dad had studied twenty-five years earlier.

Everything was falling into place quite splendidly. It seemed we were finally becoming established in London and building our new life together. But after these productive few years of assiduously climbing ladders to get away from my origins, I was about to go sliding down the longest snake on the board.

Mom came to visit us soon after we moved into the condominium. She wanted some help understanding a word processing course she was taking and also brought us up to date with what was happening in her life. One evening, while I was sitting quietly on the loveseat in our living room and Vince and Catherina were in the kitchen, Mom suddenly came gliding through the adjoining dining room. She was giddy, quickly dancing in circles as she made her way toward me while singing a weird tune. I tensed up, wondering what strange mental zone she was in and steeling myself to take the situation in hand and get her to lie down when, all of a sudden, she came to a stop right in front of me. She fell to her knees and forcefully burrowed her head deep into my lap while pushing my legs apart.

I recoiled from this creepy waking nightmare, grabbed her by the arms, and pushed her away, asking, "What on earth are you doing, Mom? Stop it! Just leave me alone!"

Vince and Catherina heard the alarm in my voice and came quickly into the living room, but they didn't know what had just happened or what to do. Hoping that all of this could be explained as just another insulin reaction, I immediately mixed her some orange juice and sugar and prompted her to drink it. I waited for her to settle down, and it then became clear that she didn't recall any part of what had just happened. Desperately hoping that all of this could be rationally explained away, the hauntingly vivid sexual nightmares from my childhood flashed through my mind, including those strange dreams of demons prancing around my parents' bed. But this time it was my mom who had just pranced around me, and I was thoroughly disgusted by the conviction that this was not the first time she had violated me.

Right after Mom left, I all but collapsed for a few weeks. I felt too weak to write or think or physically move. My nerves felt like they were shaking and burning. I just couldn't be sure if Mom's bizarre behavior had triggered a real memory of sexual abuse from my childhood. Following doctor's orders, for the first time in my life I actually took a vacation of sorts and slowed down, giving my mind and body a chance to recover from the stress it took to leave my family and get established in London. It was a troubled rest, a rocky idle. I was plagued with suspicions about what had really happened in my deepest past and was equally unsettled by premonitions of calamities to come.

Mom visited again later that summer. She and Dad had finally worked out the details of their divorce. Mom shared with me what finally precipitated the break. She'd met another Christian man, Al, at the Miami airport while visiting with her sister. It was an instant connection as they shared their United Pentecostal roots, and they exchanged phone numbers and promised to keep in touch. She adored his eye contact, frank honesty, and responsibility; and he accepted her health conditions and the limitations those would bring. Mom had also been seeing a pastor to get advice on divorce and remarriage, and because of her sham of a marriage with Dad, he was encouraging her to go ahead with her relationship with Al. I too felt that the divorce was essential for Mom's well being but feared she was rushing way too fast into remarriage.

Vince and I later met Al, and he was clearly a man who loved her and was willing to take care of her. She soon moved to Florida to begin her new life and prepare for her upcoming marriage. She shared only limited information with Al about what she had lived through in Canada. They were married in Miami in early April of 1988 with all of her children in attendance. All of Al's children were there as well. Al only knew that my father liked men, but he didn't know about the various traumatic experiences that had occurred, and his children knew absolutely nothing about any of it.

Mom was dressed in a satiny ivory dress and matching shoes, and I stood next to her as her matron of honor. We had some quiet time to talk while she applied translucent powder to her face in the upstairs' washroom. Mom was very stressed, and her blood sugar level was not controllable. I made sure she had some sugar water and something to eat, but she seemed out of sorts during the wedding ceremony, though I don't think anyone else picked up on the cues for which I had been watching since I was very young.

My feelings were so mixed that day. I knew she needed someone to really love and take care of her. In a hundred ways, she deserved that like no one else in this world. And Al was a good man prepared to stand by her come what may. She would experience satisfaction with Al that had never been possible with Dad. Not the least of these would be the pleasure of making her home and placing her furniture wherever she pleased. Dad's different boyfriends had always had first say on decorating in our house. Even after Mom moved into her own condominium in Toronto before marrying Al, Dad still had the final say on furniture placement and decorating options. I just felt Mom needed time to adjust, to find herself, and to recover from the last debacle of a marriage before hurling herself into the next one.

Back in Canada, Vince and I visited Dad in a deli restaurant in Toronto. He was dressed in comfortable gray sweatpants and a top, seated next to Ron. His demeanor seemed slightly different, more fragile somehow. Possibly, the reality of the divorce was sinking in. I think he was beginning to see how his life was sailing by, and how his children had all grown up and were finding their way in the world without him. His life was moving into one of its later phases, and he still wasn't satisfied. He'd lost a lot of partners and friends over the years and must have felt lonely. I believe he had begun to miss me, in some respects, more than he ever thought he would.

He'd lost a lot of weight. His clothes hung loosely on his frame, and he didn't seem to be his old vibrant self. His eyes looked glazed and sunken, as if they held secrets he dared not speak. I tried to be sensitive, touching his arm and hand, leaning toward him, and listening attentively while stealing some glances at Ron. Ron seemed overprotective of my dad, as if he were sick. They had become monogamous now that Dad was slowing down. Dad no longer had the strength to cruise or venture out through the shopping districts of Yorkville as he once had enjoyed doing. Convinced that Dad was hiding something important from me, I began to intuit that he was dying of AIDS.

I had met an older, successful businesswoman, Elizabeth, through the church. Elizabeth had racked up three failed marriages, attracting one man after another, each of whom turned out to be an abusive alcoholic creep. I could relate like mad to this older woman who'd been to the pit and back. She reminded me of Mary Magdalene. I was comfortable with her, knowing she wouldn't be easily intimidated by the kinds of horrendous secrets I carried. We regularly met for coffee at a London café and talked a lot on the telephone. She just listened and was there for me, and I trusted her instincts and valued her opinions and suggestions.

Elizabeth had the kind of tenacity that had helped her overcome everything life threw at her, and I valued her as a crusty mentor in the Christian life. Her easy sympathy and interest offered me a safe place to share worries about Dad's health and concerns of my own. When I mentioned that I thought Dad might be dying of AIDS, she empathized, leaned over, and touched my hand. I asked her, "Will you be there for me when my father dies?" Her immediate response was, "Of course." She promised not to tell anyone about my family situation. She never judged me or gossiped. She was a true image-bearer of Christ.

One Sunday afternoon in early 1988, I was suddenly compelled to phone my father. I had just seen a man on a television news clip who looked eerily like him, lying on his side in a Toronto hospital ward and wearing an oxygen mask over his face. The reporter was describing the respiratory illnesses that often plague those with jeopardized immunity and AIDS. I knew Dad had been hospitalized recently and was having difficulty breathing.

The phone rang and Dad answered, "Hello."

I hesitated and then I spoke to him what was in my heart. "Dad, how are you?"

His reply was harsh and cold. "Why are you calling me right now?" he asked in an annoyed voice, as if I was interrupting something.

I told him I had suddenly felt that he was somehow in danger.

"Don't bug me about such stupidity. Are you out of your mind?"

It was then I said, "All that is hidden is going to be revealed. All that is in the darkness is going to be brought to the light."

Unnerved, he hung up on me.

I was scarcely less unnerved myself. I didn't know why I had burst out with such words except I sensed that I was fighting a demonic presence that was somehow related to my father. This was totally out of character for me; I had never crossed Dad quite like this before, having always sought to be compliant toward him.

Later that night, after Vince had gone to work, I was getting ready to sleep when I felt prompted by the Holy Spirit to open my

Bible to Matthew 10. Not understanding why, I did so and read the very words I had spoken to Dad. I was astonished and prayed for a while. I had just turned off my lamp on the cherry wood night table to go to sleep when I felt prompted to turn the light back on and read Matthew 10:26–27 (NIV) again: "So do not be afraid of them. There is nothing concealed that will not be disclosed, or hidden that will not be made known. What I tell you in the dark, speak in the daylight; what is whispered in your ear, proclaim from the roofs."

Scripture was telling me not to be afraid of anything that would be revealed in the days ahead. I sensed that my father was struggling to turn toward God and prayed that this was so. And I realized that if I was praying that Dad would reach out to God, then I needed to reach out from under to Dad as well. I wanted resolution on so many issues and sensed he was more ill than he wanted me to know.

We began talking to each other like never before. We would run up many thousands of dollars in long distance charges during the last five years of his life. I was determined to finally get that deep relationship with him based on love that I had yearned for all my life. We also started exchanging letters. He would thank me for recent letters or phone calls and sign off by expressing his love with a trail of x's and o's. It was the kind of sign off you'd expect from a thirteen-year-old in the grip of puppy love. But I wasn't about to give up on Dad, realizing he hadn't known the kind of love he finally seemed to want to express to me.

In another letter, he expressed strong admonition, in red ink, for me to vote for Christian principles in an upcoming election. Was he finally turning toward Jesus Christ? In September of 1988,

I learned that Dad had accepted the Lord. That was the good news. The not-so-good news was that this acceptance had been mediated by the disgraced televangelist Jimmy Swaggart who had recently been caught purchasing the services of a prostitute and whose tear-faced confession of sin made it into newspapers and news broadcasts throughout the English-speaking world. Dad clearly forgave Swaggart for this lapse and even may have been especially attracted to him thereby. They had some sexual indiscretions they shared as men.

Possibly, Dad couldn't find a local community of believers with whom to fellowship and receive biblical teaching about forgiveness and making amends. I don't know too many homosexuals or ex-homosexuals who would find church the most comfortable and accommodating place where they could open up, share about themselves, and be accepted.

There are glaring inadequacies in any organization like Swaggart's. Without the personal connection of a small, community-based church, they can't fully, personally minister to people. And the ravenous need for funding from any source at all makes them compromise their own core principles. I had seen Dad's salesmanship up close, racking up commissions while recruiting the top sales managers for large corporations and competing with other Toronto recruiting agencies. I couldn't help but suspect that no small part of the appeal of the Swaggart organization for Dad was its business savvy.

Also, Dad's predilection for the glitzy and the flashy would have made him balk at the prospect of taking his place in a more traditional parish community. Before linking up with Swaggart, he'd been attracted to Toronto's first evangelical super-church,

The Prayer Palace, a sprawling razzmatazz operation situated in the Jane/Finch corridor of strip malls, auto dealerships, and low-income housing projects. In a sanctuary decked out with plastic palm trees and a see-through Lucite lectern, a team of pastors delivered marathon-length motivational sermons, the peppiness of the proceedings driven home by an eight-piece praise band and a thirty-member choir.

I believe Dad was sincere in reaching out to God. He was a walking dead man by this point and knew it, even if he wouldn't share that knowledge with us. I tremble to contemplate the magnitude of his fears and regrets as he looked back over a life that was about to end. And with his customary energy now sapped by disease, I believe he settled for the easiest, quickest spiritual fix he could find. I lament that, but it is not for me to judge it.

To my knowledge, Dad didn't receive any biblical instruction, but within a few months of his salvation experience, he was placed within a leadership position in Jimmy Swaggart Ministries and was regularly cutting Swaggart checks to the tune of thousands of dollars per month. Is it just filial loyalty and love that makes me think that as bad and superficial as this arrangement looks, it redounds much more to the discredit of Jimmy Swaggart than my dad?

One of Swaggart's ways of paying back the mightiest of his supporters was to feature their pictures and images in newsletters and pamphlets and the stationery and envelopes that the ministry issued. One of these envelopes was decorated on the right-hand side with a photograph of Dad's hand. I recognized it by the very distinctive ring on his finger and a watch. In another picture, Scott was with Ron, all shown standing among others in rows of pews. As well, there was a camp meeting brochure with Ron shown on the right-hand side when you opened it up. Scott had reconciled with Dad and gone along with him and Ron to a camp meeting of the Swaggart ministry. Just who Swaggart thought Ron was, I couldn't imagine.

Dad had set up Scott in a fully furnished condominium, outfitted with everything he could need. Dad provided clothes and gave Scott a supervisory position at his office. Scott took equivalency courses to finish high school, and received tutoring and prepared for university, where he earned his degree in a few years. This was a miraculous turn of events for Scott, a sort of variation on the prodigal son. Scott hadn't exactly left a warm, loving home. It was more like Dad's neglect and abandonment left Scott with no choice but to leave. Yet here Scott was, returning from the land of the lost, coming back and getting the royal treatment. Dad was really trying to make up for all the lost years. Possibly he'd wished for such a reunion with his own father after he left home at fifteen.

Dad let Thomas and me know that looking ahead he thought we'd probably do all right for ourselves, but he was more worried over the long term about Scott. This made both of us wonder if, perhaps, we'd overdone our appearance of sufficiency and competence. Thomas was understandably jealous about how many more favors Scott received. He had done his best as a son to obey all the rules—to finish school and make a life for himself—without being lavished upon in this way by Dad.

Certainly, Dad did amend some of his behavior following his conversion. Though he and Ron were living together in the Toronto condominium, they slept in separate rooms and began to abstain from sexual activities after Dad committed his life to Christ. Though they still resided in the heart of the gay village, they stopped going to the bars and parties, and Dad's cruising days were done.

His conversion brought more of an openness in our relationship. He shared more about his lifelong regrets and commented on his surprising change in priorities. He really regretted marrying Mom, he said, but he was glad to have three children.

"Dawn, I wanted children," he told me. "I wanted you, and I will never regret having children. You were wanted. You and your brothers were not a mistake. I do not want you to ever think differently."

This confession alone I have come to regard as the greatest gift he ever gave me. If the reopening of relations with Dad exposed me to a lot of pain as well, this one longed-for statement from him made all of it worthwhile.

He felt he had spent too much time going through business magazines and newspapers, which were not important to him anymore, he told me. He began reading his Bible regularly, writing notes in it, and listening to Christian music and videos. He paid for Vince and me to get an expensive VCR so we could watch Christian videos, and he sent along the tuition fees for a few CMA courses that I was completing. And then, he invited Vince and me to go with him to "Camp Meeting 1988" in Baton Rouge, Louisiana, the annual jamboree held by Jimmy Swaggart Ministries.

Just before the meeting, Vince and I went to Toronto to visit Dad and firm up the details of our trip. We saw him in his new office suite where he'd finally attained his heart's desire: a corner office with a window facing Bloor Street. He had more than twenty employees now. The consultants, he had bragged to me, were grossing over $200,000 per annum, minimum. Things had never been better financially for him, as he received a cut of every commission as president and part owner of the national company. Stepping into this domain, everything looked expensive—from the dark wood desk to the sumptuous leather couch. Dad greeted us sitting up on this couch and stretching as though he had just awakened. Dad had been a practitioner of the short power nap for as far back as I could remember, but this one didn't seem to have revived him so much as those earlier ones had.

I hesitantly asked him, "Dad, can I please sit…in your office chair?"

He nodded his agreement and smiled. I respectfully stepped past him and around his desk, grabbed the back of his chair, and felt its value and weight as I rolled it out to take a seat. The firm plush was exquisitely comfortable. It was a moment out of time as I looked at Dad and thought, *You've worked all your life to arrive at this point. Now, you're dying, and you won't be able to enjoy it after all.*

It all looked so imposing and permanent, but on that particular day, I could feel it all dissolving like snow in rain. Perhaps he read my mind. Almost casually as he looked out the window, Dad asked if I would ever go to the AIDS Memorial if his name was on it. Still not looking straight at me, I could feel the intensity with which he awaited my reaction.

"Of course, I would go," I told him. This hypothetical reference was as close as he ever came to telling me he was dying.

"Here," he said, changing the subject and handing me his credit card and scribbling out a permission note for me to use it. "I want you to get some nice clothes to go to Baton Rouge." He told me not to worry about the cost. On the way out, I got a final tour of his office and chatted with the staff.

I went down the elevator and moved through the marble halls of the main floor lobby. I was off on my shopping excursion and really didn't know where to start. Vince came with me as I checked out the best women's clothiers on Bloor Street. In one store, I saw a price tag for eight hundred dollars for a jacket and skirt set. It was beautiful, but I never could bear to spend that kind of money on just one outfit. So I left and headed to Fairweather's, where I found eight different outfits—from skirts to jackets to dresses—and bought them all for around five hundred dollars. I was happy with this. It was the only time in my life I ever had had the opportunity to spend this kind of money on myself.

Soon we met up with Dad again. This time, we were shopping for suits for the guys. Each of my brothers and Vince got measured for pants and jackets in an expensive clothier in the vicinity of Dad's new office. He spared no expense. These suits were made of the finest threads and carried well-respected labels. We next shopped for leather shoes and belts and tailor-made shirts. When it was my turn to go into a shoe store called Bally's, we dropped another six hundred dollars on ivory colored shoes with a matching purse.

It was all so surreal. Never before had I enjoyed this kind of opportunity. I profusely thanked Dad and hugged him as we loaded all this gear into our car for the drive back to London. I admit it; my head was swimming with the mercantile extravagance of it all. Vince, on the other hand, was unimpressed. He knew it was pointless to make waves with Dad and had simply gone along for the ride. A new suit of clothes wouldn't change his sense of himself, but I was not so impervious to a sartorial overhaul.

I knew appearances for Dad were everything. This was a game I had played since I was a little girl. Deep down, I knew why all this fuss was being made. It wasn't about me or Vince or my brothers. Dad wanted to make the best possible impression on Jimmy

Swaggart. He wanted all of us to look as if we had money and that he took good care us. I wasn't going to argue with Dad's wishes when they coincided so neatly with my own vanity and when I knew that he wouldn't be here much longer.

And then the big day came. Vince and I had to get going in the wee hours to catch a shuttle to the Toronto Airport, where we met Dad at the unthinkable hour of five a.m. There we soon linked up with my brothers. Thomas had married a year and half earlier and was there with his wife. Scott, the prodigal son, was acting as if everything was all right—just like he always had while growing up.

Ron was not with us on this trip, and this was really unusual for Dad. It seemed that Dad's need for a man was being met in Jimmy as the current centerpiece of his life. Dad was dressed casually in blue jeans, a T-shirt, a leather coat, and a light carry-on bag. His health had been up and down, so it was good he seemed to have some strength that day. He'd need it to get through a long day's relay of connecting flights and stopovers.

We finally arrived in Baton Rouge that night and got a sleek, white Cadillac rental car at the airport to take us to the Hilton, one of the best hotels in town.

We immediately headed into the lobby, where we were introduced to Jimmy and Frances Swaggart before heading up to our rooms. According to Dad, the Swaggarts were staying in the penthouse suite on the top floor. Frances's hair was perfect, and her attire and grooming were impeccable. Jimmy wore the traditional dark suit, dress shirt, and tie. He looked older than on television, but he had a way about him that was endearing the longer you spent time with him. His hair was thinner in real life and looked almost gelled back in place. His eyes were deep, framed by circles underneath and deeply set wrinkles from too much sun.

I shook their hands and said hello. They seemed like nice people, but I can't say that I fully trusted them. Jimmy had a very slick quality about him, and I could tell this was a man who knew how to work a room. In spite of my mixed feelings toward them, this couple radiated star power. I wondered if Swaggart knew about my dad's sexuality. I knew Jimmy talked with Dad almost every week and that this comforted Dad, but I doubted they shared much personal information. Swaggart went on the record several years later, expressing only contempt for homosexuals. In a September 12, 2004, worship service telecast, Swaggart said he'd kill any gay man who looked at him romantically. Swaggart was discussing his opposition to gay marriage when he said, "I've never seen a man in my life I wanted to marry. And I'm going to be blunt and plain: If one ever looks at me like that, I'm going to kill him and tell God he died." His congregation received this statement with spontaneous laughter and applause. Would my father have been surprised to hear such a contemptible sentiment expressed by this man he so admired? Probably not. Rather, I expect Dad took pains to make sure Swaggart never knew enough about him to occasion such an outburst.

I wondered why Swaggart had given Dad a national executive designation in his Canadian ministry that another high-profile television evangelist and pastor badly wanted. Was it just my dad's money and the aura of affluence that he always portrayed? Or did Swaggart genuinely care about his spiritual growth? As much as Dad esteemed Swaggart and loved the atmosphere and music at the church, I worried that he was just being professionally fleeced.

At this point in Dad's life, he was dangerously vulnerable, craving acceptance and a sense of belonging in an ultimate way before taking leave of this life altogether. I have little doubt that what he was seeking in Jimmy Swaggart was a father figure. And I expect that Swaggart left him about as frustrated in that search for affirmation of his worth as a son and a man as my dad in turn frustrated me in my quest to be affirmed as a daughter and a woman. That kind of bone-deep knowledge and security can only be bestowed by a father—or a father figure—who really knows his child and allows himself to be known as well.

Repeatedly during our six days in Baton Rouge, I would see just how superficial my father's connection was to this place he loved so much that he told me—propped up by pillows and ingesting all manner of special medicines and pills—"I would really like to die here, Dawn."

During our first full day in Baton Rouge, we got a tour of the ministry's associated buildings by the president of Jimmy Swaggart Bible College. Dad mentioned that if he wanted to get his name on one of those buildings, he'd have to contribute a few million dollars. At the Family Worship Center one afternoon, Dad stepped away for some time for the taping of a Father's Day program that would eventually air in 1991. Precious few minutes of this special Father's Day program were devoted to anything other than fundraising, and few men on this planet were less qualified to pass on insights and tips about sound parenting than Dad. But he looked good, and all of his screwed-up children were with him in Baton Rouge, so Dad got to share his nuggets of fatherly wisdom. Dad was actually feeling quite weak that day, but not wanting to disappoint anyone, he went ahead with this farcical deception, while we kept busy looking at the record, tape, and sheet-music tables. Merchandise was absolutely everywhere.

After the taping, Dad joined us in the shop. "What do you think of this jewelry?" he asked. He'd picked out a gaudy JESUS brooch, the capital letters formed in cut glass jewels, that he'd noticed a number of the more ostentatious ladies wearing. I got one of those, and he picked up another for my mother-in-law as a gift. Then he asked if I wanted some sheet music. I came over and we picked out three songbooks: *100 Favorites Jimmy Swaggart Songbook, Jimmy Swaggart Heaven's Jubilee Songbook*, and *Great Hymns of the Church by Jimmy Swaggart*. Pathetically enough, I was thankful for these items, as I took great pleasure in having some time alone with Dad, even if we wasted it in sorting through Jimmy Swaggart trinkets and mementos. At least he was next to me and I was getting some attention from him.

We had preferential seating at the camp meetings, and at one service, Dad was specially called up to the platform for prayer. After the last of the strenuously scheduled "camp meeting" sessions, we finally got to meet Jimmy and Frances in a more relaxed setting. At a quaint restaurant, the royal couple were quietly received and led to a reserved place at the head table flanked by his most generous supporters. It was strange and sad to watch Jimmy and Frances together. You could tell that they were very private people who weighed every word that came out of their mouths. I respected their politeness and reserved manner, yet I wondered how he still could be ministering after what had happened so very publicly.

To either side of Jimmy and Frances sat a pastor and his wife and other high muckety-mucks in the organization—some of whom I'd seen earlier that year on TV when Swaggart had made his tearful confession about his involvement with a prostitute. We also took our place at this long table, Dad sitting almost directly across from Jimmy and Frances.

With all he had gone through recently in the way of scandal, I couldn't help being impressed by Swaggart's nerve in appearing before us in this way. I don't think many of us still could stand up after enduring that much ridicule and humiliation. Many of his followers had taken the incident with the prostitute as their cue to leave the church. It was obviously a difficult time for him and his family. I understood by watching him that he never would allow himself to say much around us. He and Dad had a similar gift for drawing people in to their way of thinking without revealing their own hand.

Dad leaned forward at one point and asked Jimmy, "Do you think I should continue my drugs or not?" Dad was thinking about placing himself solely on the mercy of God and hoping for a miraculous healing.

Wisely, Jimmy, who knew diddly-squat about Dad's illness, didn't make a recommendation either way.

After the meal was served, Jimmy got up and deferentially went around our table, offering iced tea to each person. I wondered why he was doing this. What were his motives? Was he just making a humble and gracious gesture of thanks to his most loyal supporters? Or were we supposed to interpret his actions as Christ-like, a sort of genteel Louisiana variation on Christ's washing of His disciples' feet in the Upper Room? Like so much else about this weeklong meeting, this farewell gesture left my feelings torn neatly in two.

On the one hand, I was glad Dad had found a spiritual home that seemed to give him some sort of solace during what I more and more clearly understood were his final days. But how I wished that home had been one that would really minister to a Christian in such desperate straits as he was, where the focus was more on Christ than on this deeply flawed messenger with an insatiable need to raise cash. At this perilous time in his life, Dad needed a church where they cast aside the faux diamond brooch and esteemed the crown of thorns instead. Where followers didn't just read along from their overpriced Jimmy Swaggart songbooks but confessed and repented of those sins that most troubled their hearts. Where they didn't sit around swilling iced drinks but washed themselves clean in the waters of salvation.

The meal finished, Jimmy and Frances rose and were ushered out of the dining room, surrounded by a protective phalanx of their closest supporters. As our party got up to leave, I couldn't help noticing that Dad looked about as happy and serene as I'd ever seen him, and I felt like a heel for entertaining such doubts. I realized once again that however mixed my feelings were about this place, it was not for me to pass judgment on the form of worship my father chose. My only obligation was to pray for him, and this I continued to do over the final months of his life.

The End of the Pier

Dad and I telephoned and wrote to one another constantly and visited as we could, especially around Christmas. For our final Christmas dinner, Dad could barely walk and couldn't handle much solid food. I supplied the dessert—red Jell-O—for the table of this man who had always prided himself on the sophistication of his palate and eating well. For a gift, my brothers and I had pitched in to have a lavender cashmere blanket made for Dad, especially embroidered with our names. Thomas had chosen the color, which made me cringe a little, lavender being to gays what green is to the Irish. Wasn't Dad trying to distance himself a little from that association—or at least downplay its importance in his life?

Dad's letters were invariably written out on special Jimmy Swaggart stationery. Though still living with Ron, who gave Dad wonderful and attentive care all through his losing battle with AIDS, Dad had ceased all sexual relations. Dad didn't tell me this; Scott did. In our final conversations, whether written or spoken,

Dad reflected on his life and shared his feelings like never before, recognizing that a lot of the problems he had never faced up to were spiritual in nature.

He deeply abhorred the abuse he had endured as a child and his toxic relationship with his father. He estimated that he had been molested and sodomized at least a hundred times before running away from home at the age of fifteen. While no one would condemn him for running away from such hell, he knew that his leaving only left other family members, like Bea, at the mercy of an utterly merciless beast. And I think he saw that his running away had also established the pattern of abandonment by which he in turn would bring so much pain to so many others. The list of those he had wounded included not only his wife and children, but also a string of discarded homosexual lovers; some of whom had come to rely on him so completely that they killed themselves rather than face life without him.

Vastly improved as our relationship was in those final days, not everything could be repaired. This was partly due to a long learned reticence on my part. As Dad shared with me about the horror and humiliation of the abuse he had suffered as a child, it might have seemed that here was a natural opening to discuss the abuse and perversion that had blighted my childhood as well. I broached the subject of physical discipline—the beatings Mother had administered with the belts and sticks he'd brought into our home—and he feigned ignorance that any such punishment had ever been carried out, assuring me that he would have stopped it if only he'd known. I didn't believe his denial for a second, but I did believe it was what he badly wanted to believe.

Dad was so very fragile in both body and spirit at this time that I let it go. If he wasn't prepared to meet me halfway in candor regarding the reality of life in our home, I knew I only risked provoking an argument or hurting his feelings. There was no way I was going to plant myself on the wrong side of this man who had always held such power over me. Nor was I going to risk losing this new access to and openness with my dad. Even if it wasn't entirely honest, even if it didn't make it possible to shine a light in some of the darkest corners of our lives, this new atmosphere between us of caring and support was something I'd been craving from birth. With twenty-eight years of deprivation to make up for, I intended to enjoy this while I could.

During his final spring, Dad's medical treatment and his own rallying constitution briefly restored him to an approximation of his customary energy and health. It was horribly disheartening then to see him revert to some of his old immoral and interfering ways. Was it only the prospect of death that made Dad a better person? Or were the drugs, perhaps, affecting his judgment? I would prefer to believe the latter.

I was stressed out at this time to the max. Distracted by Dad's impending death, I was also struggling to keep my head above water in one of the most ill-equipped and mean-spirited offices in which it's ever been my misfortune to work. Dad knew how much I hated this job and how bitterly I clung to it, as finances were so tight just then at home. Early one weekday, he called through to me at work. He'd been up half the night and worked out a scheme that would solve all my problems. My current job was doomed, he said. I was going to lose it, and indeed I did just that, precisely two weeks later. What I had to do, he said, was make a clean break from everything that was dragging me down.

These weren't just recommendations he was making. They were orders. I should leave Vince immediately and start arrangements for our divorce. And he said Jimmy Swaggart thought so too. Vince was a loser who was holding me back from the sort of economic comforts that were mine by birthright. This was the same sort of thing I'd heard from my mother and brothers in the past as well, but I'd thought Dad and I recently had moved onto a new plateau of respect for one another. Apparently not. I should leave London and our home and our church, he said, and move back to Toronto, where Dad would help me get an apartment and establish myself in a whole new life. And if I didn't go along with this eminently sensible plan he'd just hatched, Dad said he would cut me off financially. He was through cutting the occasional check to help us meet our phone bills, and if I didn't do as he said, he would also cut me out of his will.

I was shattered by this ultimatum. Not for one second did I consider doing as he said, but all the progress we'd made in the previous couple of years seemed to evaporate with his spiteful words. Less than an hour later, he called me back with a reprieve, but his voice was still laced with bitterness. In the time since our last talk, he actually had called through to Baton Rouge to see what the Great One thought about his plan. In a disappointed tone of voice he said, "I just got off the phone with Jimmy Swaggart, and he told me you cannot get a divorce. It wouldn't be right. So forget that."

Right-ee-oh, Dad. If Jimmy says so, then I'll just forget every hateful thing you said to me. This latest twist only deepened my depression.

Within his own heart, by his own lights, Dad couldn't find any reason to honor the fact that I loved Vince, had given myself to him, and intended to stand by him. Nor did he bother to mention whether or not I was back in his good graces. I rather doubted I was, but there was no way I was going to ask, "So if I don't have to leave Vince after all, does that mean I'm back in your will?"

When I got home that night, I told Vince about the phone calls. He was understandably angry at first, and then appalled, but he quickly arrived at a position on all this that confirmed for me what a good man he was. "Dawn, your father isn't in his right mind," Vince said with a charity and calm that I still couldn't muster, and I hadn't even been the one Dad had primarily slimed. Sure, he'd disregarded my integrity and my feelings, but he hadn't said I was a hopeless prospect who only deserved to be tossed overboard and fed to the sharks. "Can't you see?" Vince said. "The AIDS and the drugs are taking some awful toll on him. This isn't him talking. We've got to forgive this." And so we did.

Soon Dad was feeling worse again as the illness took hold with renewed ferocity and never let go this side of the grave. This final illness he would never admit was AIDS related. It was cancer. Just plain cancer. He became so weakened that during our last visits, I was not allowed to get too close to him in case I might expose him to germs against which he had no defense. Before eating or drinking anything, he or Ron would carefully wipe the plates and glassware clean. His strength was zapped from his body by the slightest exposure to any bacterial or viral pests in the air or on surfaces.

Aggressive Kaposi's Sarcoma—a condition causing cancerous malignant tumors that inflict those with suppressed immunity systems—had invaded Dad's body for the final battle. These cancerous lesions exploded all over, causing purplish, grape-like growths to fester all over his face, back, arms, thighs, and feet. It also moved into his gastrointestinal tract, lungs, and other internal organs, causing him an immense amount of pain while eating and drinking, making him short of breath, and setting off fits of coughing. Though he had endured intense radiation and chemotherapy treatments—which themselves caused severe headaches, nausea, and vomiting—this time there was no holding back the tide.

In Dad's last letter to me, his script is so crabbed with pain it is almost illegible. "I do apologize for not calling as often, but the cancer is having a heyday," he wrote. "I am seeking the Master with my very energies, since some of the new treatments are most painful. I might be bedridden for a couple of months, during the radiation on my feet. Please seek the will of God for my life. Although I want to see the One who pours His Spirit through me two or three times weekly—my family are not all in the fold and hell is very real. Oh, that they might know Him in the power of His resurrection. Pardon my handwriting, but the afternoon has been not good… Dawn, He's all we need, Jesus is all we need. I love Him beyond words. He, Jesus, broke my bondage and set me free. He gave me a starving hunger for His Spirit. I need Him so very much. I must close to get this in the mail. Your dad in Christ. XXOO."

On October 10, 1991, I saw my father for the last time. Recognizing that Dad was not his biggest fan and not wanting to interfere with what we feared could be my last conversation with Dad, Vince waited for me in the car.

Opening the door to me with a heartbroken expression on his face, Ron quietly sat me down on the green leather couch to prepare me for the shock of Dad's appearance and to caution me to be as gentle as possible. Ron suddenly flinched as Dad cried out in a pain-drenched moan from the next room. Gesturing that I should stay put, Ron quickly rose and went to pump more morphine through the tube into my father's veins.

I always had resented Ron and all the other boyfriends who had come between Dad and me. Our relationship would never be warm, but watching Ron race through to ease Dad's pain, I was immensely grateful he was there and tending to him in a tireless, selfless way. No one else in our family could bear or be bothered to take on this task. Mom hadn't seen Dad in at least three years and already had told me she wouldn't be attending his funeral. Sure, she had the excuse of living in Florida with her new husband, and I lived in London with Vince, and my brothers had their own families and lives to be getting on with. But when push came to shove and better came to worse and ruddy health came to agonizing sickness, the only person who really stood by Dad in a minute-by-minute way was Ron. Over the course of fourteen years, he had turned out to be something much sturdier and finer than just another joy boy.

Once the morphine started to muffle his pain, I went to Dad's bedroom. The first thing I noticed was how thin he had become. His face was sullen and his eyes sunken and dim, as if covered by translucent lids. He could no longer walk. Under layers of blankets and covers I could see the outline of his now useless legs, buckled up at the knees. He was in an incredible amount of pain, as the AIDS cancelled all immunity to the cancer that ravaged his body. The doctors had wanted to amputate one of his feet, but Dad adamantly refused to let that happen. He was not going to take leave of life one piece at a time.

Dad lay there all but motionless except for the slight rise and fall of his chest and the blinking of his eyes, which scarcely seemed to notice who was in the room. I wanted to touch his pale and slender hands. "Can I touch your hands?" I asked, as I tentatively reached out. "Do you mind if I do?"

"Yes," he barely whispered through cracked lips, the usual ambiguity hovering in the air between us. *Yes, I can touch them? Or, yes, you mind?* I gently laid my hands on his, and they didn't move or pull away. I could feel the tissue-paper thinness and coolness of his skin and the frail bones just beneath. Here was the man whose attention I'd always longed to hold for long enough that we could talk. Finally, he was still and not turning away or trying to get out the door to be with someone else, but I couldn't communicate with him anymore. Knowing someone was with him but unsure who, he called out, "Is this my daughter?"

"Yes, Daddy, it is," I said.

"Is this my daughter?" he repeated, as though he hadn't heard me. "Tell her that I love her."

Those precious, longed-for words had finally been spoken. About me, yes. But not to me. Did it make such a difference that his expression of love was mediated? Was I so well trained in cruel paternal disappointment that I couldn't receive his words as nourishment for my soul? Didn't it amount to the same thing, however he'd phrased it? I didn't know the answer to these questions yet. I only knew that my father—this man I'd both feared and by whom I'd longed to be loved all of my life—had already and irreversibly moved beyond my reach.

"Will you come with me to the end of the pier?" he'd asked me nearly twenty years before, setting off explosions of fear and uncertainty in my heart. I'd been swallowing that fear all of my life, trying to stay as close to him as I could, starved for whatever morsels of nourishment he could throw my way. Whatever damage had been done, whatever restitution we had lately made, whatever chasms between us had remained unbridgeable, and whatever words were left unspoken, this was as far as we could go together along that pier. As he had taken my photograph and then word-lessly walked away that distant summer day, I now looked around his room through tear-brimmed eyes, drinking in every detail I could during these last moments with my father on this earth. I was so moved and so grateful to see that the painting I'd given him of a becalmed sailboat was still hanging on the wall by the door. Perhaps it would be—or already had been—the last thing he saw. I prayed that the same kind of serenity depicted there was what awaited him as he moved on alone beyond the end of the pier. He would be dead in less than twenty-four hours, dying at nine p.m. on the eve of Thanksgiving Day at the age of fifty-one.

Scott phoned with the news of Dad's death as Thomas, Vince, and I were heading to our aunt's and uncle's for a Thanksgiving feast. It so happened that Vince and I already had booked some time off work, leaving us free to give ourselves over to what would be a week of enormous repercussions and revelations. Thomas made a series of calls to the funeral home, badgering them to tell us the cause of Dad's death. He batted aside one concealing lie af-ter another until they finally came clean and spoke the "A" word. In our heart of hearts we'd known it was AIDS all along, but this objective confirmation of the fact still had the power to make my thoughts reel.

AIDS at that time still carried an enormous stigma. Polite company would back away if you mentioned the word. Many people were still so ignorant of the disease and how it was spread that they'd decline to shake hands or give an embrace of consolation when they learned how Dad had died. Sad to say, one of the very worst environments of superstition and denial about AIDS was the church. I phoned my older Mary Magdalene-type friend, Elizabeth, and got her to impart the news to my pastor, but I knew better than to hold my breath waiting for any expression of acknowledgment or sympathy from him, and indeed, none came.

Thomas was as heartbroken as I was, but poking through his grief those first couple of days was a palpable, shimmering rage. Away from our relatives and back at Thomas's apartment on Thanksgiving night, Vince and I were alarmed to find that he'd kicked in one of his closet doors in a stupefying rage, breaking it away from its hinges and reducing it to splinters. Thomas was much more plugged in to Dad's financial standing than I was. He had what would turn out to be a pretty accurate hunch that between the grasping machinations of the Jimmy Swaggart organization and the position of favoritism that Scott and Ron had cultivated over the last few years, he would be all but cut out of the will.

I knew that Dad and Thomas had had a pretty complete falling out when Thomas held that executive recruiting position and went head to head against Dad for commissions. In one of our last lucid conversations, Dad told me he thought Thomas was way too materialistic. As usual, I hadn't had the courage to say, "Ah, Dad, I wonder where he got that from?" Nor did I ask if there were "any other charges that the pot would care to lay against the kettle at this time." It was useless to point out hypocrisy or contradictions in Dad's behavior. He was impervious to logic or consistency. At the very same time Dad was ragging Thomas for only wanting money, he was dumping on me for not wanting it—advising me to ditch my husband and the life we'd made together so I could get on the moolah-earning fast track without any boring human impediments.

That last night at Dad's condo, Ron mentioned to me that Thomas had been making rather desperate overtures within Dad's final week, expressing anger about being mistreated and pushed aside. He wanted the same due consideration I had been after. Clearly, Thomas had begun such reparations too late, which no doubt fueled some of his door-demolishing rage. Tucking down that night with Vince, we talked over the prospect of the will. Having no real confidence how things might shake down, I vowed to Vince, "Whatever Dad's estate gives me, I will split it right down the middle with Thomas if he doesn't get anything."

The very night Dad died, his hero Jimmy Swaggart was caught in his second dalliance with a prostitute. The immediate scandal attending this second lapse cancelled any hope that the Great One would be giving the eulogy at Dad's funeral, and he sent up one of his underlings instead; a man who knew even less about Dad than Jimmy did.

Prior to the service when the casket was still open, Thomas came up to me and said, "Dad must be cold. I've got that blanket we gave him for Christmas. Why don't we all go up and place it on him?"

My mixed feelings about the lavender blanket aside, that quiet moment when Dad's three children stood together in silent prayer and grief resides in my memory as the only pure gesture or tribute in the entire service. Once the lid on the casket was sealed, Dad—as inappropriate in death as in life—had a dozen virginal white roses set on top. The speech delivered by Jimmy's underling—praising Dad's philanthropy to the Swaggart Ministry and scarcely acknowledging the existence of anything else in Dad's life—was pathetic.

After the interment ceremony at the cemetery, the siblings, their spouses, and Ron went with Swaggart's lieutenant for dinner at a restaurant. This insensitive oaf of a man tried to lighten our moods by cracking some tasteless joke about adultery. When he wasn't being offensive, he was being smarmy, telling us that Jimmy would do anything to help us through this rough time. It was the kind of encounter that leaves you wanting nothing more than a cleansing shower.

A couple of weeks later we convened again, minus the Swaggart oaf, to settle the estate. In the end, Thomas and I both were allotted $50,000. It's more than a lot of children ever see from their parents' estates, and it certainly helped Vince and me pay off our mortgage and get a more secure financial footing in life. But for my higher rolling twin, $50,000 was chump change. I expect he could have happily accepted that as his due if it hadn't been for some wild disparities in how Dad chose to parcel out his fortune. Our prodigal brother, Scott, would ultimately receive fifteen times more money than we did. The Swaggart Ministry received another $200,000, pushing their lifetime take from Dad over the one-million-dollar mark. Ron received Dad's condo and all its furnishings, as well as Dad's Cadillac.

Any residue left over in the estate after the settlement was to be split between Ron and Scott. These two, partners with Dad on so many trips down to Swaggart's Baton Rouge headquarters, were the favored ones and had been left with control of Dad's company and the lion's share of his estate. Quickly discovering that Dad's little empire didn't run half as efficiently without Dad at the helm, neither one of them chose to stay with the company and even had begun selling off some of the assets as Dad lay dying, thus lowering the estate taxes that would be owed. Ultimately, the company Dad had stepparented became insolvent, leaving the company shares worthless and permanently closing its doors.

Neither Scott nor Ron stayed with the Swaggart Ministry either, nor with any other church affiliation. Ron did stay on in Dad's old condo and was soon living with another man, that relationship lasting for five years until Ron's own death from AIDS in 1996.

Three Flowers

Around the time of Dad's death, I had been finishing up my accounting courses and looking for work, and Vince had enrolled in some part-time courses at McMaster University to top up his social work credentials. In the early spring of '92, I began accompanying Vince on the ninety-minute trip to Hamilton two times a week. This was a wonderful opportunity to be alone with my husband. I loved setting off together in the pre-dawn dark, both of us sipping warm cups of flavored coffee, and inching down the window as the rising sun warmed the landscape through which we moved. These excursions represented an eight-hour slab of uninterrupted time away from the world. Nobody could reach me on those days. I was accountable to no one, and for those hours when Vince was in classes, I would make my way to a corner of the library or find a spot to sit in a sun-warmed court where I could read a book or write in my journal. Usually I wrote.

McMaster was the university Thomas and I had tried to attend as a way of getting out from under Dad's oppressive control. Now his death had swung that same prison door wide open, and I was finally free—wasn't I?—to dream about my future and chart the path I would take. Yet when it came time to uncap my pen and take my dreams for a walk, I was startled to read what came gushing onto the pages of my journal—words as ugly and violent and raw as blood from an open wound. I wasn't able to look toward the future at all but was completely ensnared by my past, as though it were some sort of metal trap. I could thrash and squirm in its grip, but I soon understood that I wouldn't be going anywhere new in my life until I found some way to pry myself free from the past.

Just writing it all down was a start. It was the same old litany— the abuse and perversion of my upbringing, the fears and depression that had dogged even my earliest childhood, the resultant confusion and uncertainty about my own sexuality. None of this was fun or pleasant to write about, but it poured out of me unstoppably; and there was within me now a new readiness to deal with it. This time, perhaps naïvely, I felt that I had a fighting chance. Whatever sense I could make of it all, whatever progress I could make toward health and truth, those advances wouldn't all be erased next week or next month with the first telephone call from or visit to my dad.

Mom was still around, but she just didn't have the same hold on my psyche. She never had, and, perhaps sadly, she never would. For one thing, she was remarried and living in Florida. She would call and we'd talk about her concerns and health worries—when I wasn't imposing a communications ban on her so I could get my studying done. But nothing she said had the power to obliterate my well being like Dad could with the merest arching of an eye-brow. As I furiously filled one spiral-bound journal after another, I found I was dealing with my parents separately, generating only one entry about Mom for every ten about Dad. She had been a weak and inconsistent mother. I knew that. She had been woefully unsupportive and even cruel when she herself couldn't cope. But I couldn't get very worked up about something I sensed had never really been her fault. All my life, I'd intuitively sensed that she was primarily a reactor and hadn't been the ultimate source of our family's misery.

I felt an excitement to finally be confronting these unspeakable secrets, even a giddy kind of liberation to finally be uncovering what had always been carefully hidden and not care much who saw what. I felt like the coroner who yanks an obscuring blanket off a mangled corpse and says, "OK, here it is in all its hideousness. Now let's try to understand what happened here."

Once a thing is written down on paper and you have to look it over, it takes on a new and insistent reality. Just in writing it all down, I realized I wouldn't be able to push it aside again. Now, I would have to address it. On the way up to McMaster each morning, we mostly talked about Vince's work. I regularly critiqued his essays and helped out by typing up a clean final draft. On the way home, Vince would return the favor by focusing more on me, making comments and suggestions on the revelations I had dragged out into the light in that day's journal writing. Though Vince knew the general tenor and extent of what I had been through, the gruesome details were new to him. And bless his heart, he never flinched. These sessions really took it out of me, and by the time we got back to London each day, the first thing I had to do was crawl off to bed for a couple of hours of profoundly deep sleep.

Vince was so patient and understanding at this time. From the day he first met me, certainly from the time of our engagement,

Vince had known that psychologically I was going to be one very high-maintenance spouse. Yet, he never pressured me to unload this dark stuff before I was ready to deal with it, nor to pack it back up and put it away once it started spewing forth in such an uncontrollable way. I have sometimes caught myself wishing Vince occasionally could be a little more intuitive, a little less predictable, or more spontaneously responsive in his interactions with me. And then I realize that those are the qualities—or the anti-qualities— that Dad constantly exhibited throughout my life and that wreaked such havoc with my development in every way. As surely as Dad's death was necessary before I could tackle the work that lay ahead, so too were the conditions of stability and dependability Vince lovingly provided.

Though unspoken at first, Vince and I both came to recognize that I was going to need some professional help with this one. I had recently made friends with a woman named Lauren who had done missions work with her husband on the island of St. Vincent. The culture shock she experienced on her return to middle-class Ontario resonated very strongly with my own sense of otherness in coming from a homosexual household. In her past, Lauren had come through some challenging circumstances from which she had extricated herself, so I perked up when she started talking about a Christian psychiatrist she'd heard speak at our church the previous Sunday. Lauren had heard good things about Dr. Blair and suggested I try him out. Vince encouraged me likewise.

Starting therapy was no easy task for me. Just a year earlier I had seen a female psychiatrist about a half-dozen times to help me deal with Dad's impending death, but we didn't probe the root causes of anything. I'm not sure I was then ready for the full process of psychoanalysis. More than anything else, I wanted a listening ear and perhaps some solid direction. But when a major part of this shrink's prognosis was to prescribe Prozac to help me cope, I soon decided to bail out. As I say, I may not have been ready yet to strap on my hip waders and go spelunking into the darkest corners of my psyche. But I intuitively sensed that no advances in self-knowledge would be achieved by slapping a few coats of medication onto my brain. So I stopped taking the pills and dropped the therapy as well.

The fact that Dr. Blair offered a Christ-centered therapy was a huge inducement to give psychiatry another try. Many forms of psychoanalysis are antagonistic to religious belief, and I wasn't about to get on board with any regimen that belittled or sought to eliminate my faith, which I knew had sustained me against daunting odds. Steeling my nerve, I phoned Dr. Blair and was relieved in a way when I was invited to leave a message on his answering machine. When they first reach out for help, many patients fear that their situations may be so hideous and disturbing that doctors will refuse them out of a healthy sense of self-preservation. To a machine, I could just spell out my predicament in all of its horror, and if Dr. Blair didn't want to risk getting involved, then he wouldn't have to get back to me.

"I need to see you," I told his machine. "I believe I may have been sexually molested as a child. I had a gay father who has since died of AIDS. And I no doubt have a lot of other issues I need to deal with as well. Please get back to me if you think you can help me with all of this." Dr. Blair did get back to me a few hours later, and we made our first appointment at his home office—a sort of sounding-each-other-out session, he told me—for later that week.

Determined to make up for lost time and to quickly get through an ordeal I saw as necessary but did not in any way savor, I booked double appointments soon after starting. I also started working on my mom. In our irregular phone calls when she shared her health woes with me and told me how cut off she felt from all of her children, I pumped her harder and harder for details on the abuse I had endured as an infant. Rather like knowing Dad was dying from AIDS even if he wouldn't admit it, I already knew the truth about the abuse in my deepest heart. There were those distressing nightmares from my childhood years of flying through the air above my parents' naked bodies and being pressed to various parts of their legs and torsos, awakening frustrating sexual feelings inside me. I knew I hadn't invented those unsettling images and sensations. Then, more recently, there had been Mom's ditzy diabetic dance, where she collapsed to the floor in front of me and in an unconscious state of raw instinct, pried my legs apart in an apparent bid to crawl inside me. What in the world was that all about? But when Mom finally did confirm my knowledge a few years after therapy, it left me both horrified and relieved.

"Yes, we did that!" she finally confessed to me in a flood of tears. "We placed you and Thomas all over our bodies. Your father liked it when you nursed at our teats."

No doubt sickened by what she was saying, Mom tried shifting all the blame onto Dad. "It was his idea," she said, as if that settled 'everything. Could no responsibility be pinned onto the equally guilty weakling who was put on this earth to protect her children but instead went along with any stupid scheme Dad cooked up for widening the lethal scope of his sex life?

Then, stooping even lower, she tried to implicate her infant twins as well. "And I might say that both of you seemed to thoroughly enjoy rubbing yourselves on us," she said. *Did we really, Mom? Could you measure our appreciation by our full, throaty laughter at the time? Or do you say this because nearly three decades later I'm still struggling with what a wonderful time we had by enduring agonizing and humiliating exchanges with a psychiatrist?*

Then, finally—and for me, most crushingly—she tried to pull the divinity sidestep. "And besides, I went to the church and asked for forgiveness about this, Dawn," she said with a tone of finality, as if no further response was possible. So she was off this particular hook, and I was still impaled on it? *Is that the way forgiveness works, Mommy? The perpetrator goes free, while the victim hangs and squirms forever? How very convenient for you.*

So yes, I had a few issues to work through as I drove up to Dr. Blair's home in a quiet neighborhood in one of the more posh areas of town for our first meeting. This neighborhood reminded me of our last family home in Forest Hill. His own house, while slightly grander in scale, had the very same tone of brown paint on the wood trim and the same fieldstone accents on its façade. Weirder yet, I would later learn that my shrink-to-be actually lived in the same section of Forest Hill for a few years that we did. We'd probably crossed paths from time to time.

When Dr. Blair came to collect me from his waiting room, I was a little unnerved by his resemblance to my dad. He was no spitting image, but he had the same blue eyes and dirty blond hair, a similar thin build and short stature. In his office, the leather couch and matching chair and ottoman put me to mind of Dad's decorating tastes, as well as the objets d'art on various tables and the book-lined shelves. With Dr. Blair, however, I knew that most of those books had actually been read.

Dr. Blair took the chair, and I landed on one end of the couch, looking around and drinking in the restful ambience of the room. There was a fireplace along one wall and large sliding patio doors that opened directly onto an enclosed and very well kept garden. Dr. Blair, only seven or eight years older than I, was still single at the time but obviously knew how to create an attractive and nurturing space—something for which a lot of men, particularly heterosexual men, don't have much of a gift. He sat back in his chair, notepad and pen in hand, and appraised me steadily with what I would come to know as the almost blink-free psychiatric stare. It wasn't threatening or intimidating, but it did make me feel a little self-conscious, which was appropriate enough, I suppose, considering the whole purpose of our work together would be to bring all aspects of myself into the full light of consciousness.

For that first session, Dr. Blair mostly gathered background information—about my family's health history on both sides (physical and mental), and our religious and ethnic background—and I gave, of course, a brief introduction to some of the psychosexual horrors of my upbringing. Growing up in such a madhouse, I'd quickly developed a defensive approach in all social situations: I only revealed as much as I comfortably could while maintaining strict control of the impression I made on others. From that very first meeting with Dr. Blair, I understood—theoretically, at least—that this tight-lipped, self-protecting approach would only defeat the whole purpose of analysis. I had to leave my desire to be in control at the door of his office. Fighting against that impulse left me feeling breathless and exposed. While Dr. Blair would make an occasional interjection that would influence the drift of my talk (scribbling away in his notepad all the while), I seemed to be doing most of the work. This is the way it has to be. For therapy to work, the patient can't be lectured or told what to do. She's got to discover her own cure for herself. Carefully and subtly guided by Dr. Blair, I spilled all the shameful secrets of my life, got them out from under and onto the table, and then started to untangle the unworkable mess they'd made of my life.

Male authority had always been an enormously difficult issue for me. I had long worried that at any time Vince would bail out on me. That's what people did in my experience, particularly men. Even with the man I married, there was a Plan B in the back of my head, just in case I had to get by without him, which I was confident I could do if necessary. Though I had not anticipated it, I now see that an essential ingredient for my successful therapy was that my psychiatrist was a man. I started out in our sessions wearing dark and shapeless clothing. As the therapy proceeded, I began wearing more distinctly feminine clothing, such as colorful dresses, and I became much more aware of my body shape. I didn't comprehend that this was a large part of my healing at the time, that acknowledging my feminine nature, coming to accept and even cherish it, was in fact the central key to my healing.

It helped very much in this process that Dr. Blair was a wonderfully kind and thoughtful man. Knowing little about his background, it was easy to idealize him. He occasionally lent books to some of his patients on subjects related to themes that came up in their therapy. And books, of course, had been the romantic currency of my very earliest exchanges with Vince. I knew Dr. Blair to be generous to all of his patients but was bowled over when he offered to cover the costs of my attending a conference in Toronto about homosexuality. I took him up on the offer and gained many insights into my father and the psychological legacy of growing up in our home, as well as the work I needed to do to repair that. Hour by hour and week by week, Dr. Blair's generosity and concern for my well being changed my view of men significantly. I finally began to believe that the masculine principle and even male authority could be forces for good in this world.

As Dr. Blair took on something like a father role to me, feelings related to my father started coming to life inside me in a most disruptive way. I wasn't just feeling rage at a father who had never been there for me or affirmed me for who I was. What was finally emerging was the flip side of all that. I was blind-sided by the powerful attractiveness of all the masculine virtues I'd never seen in our home. I was now contending with positive feelings, natural responses, and a totally new receptivity and vulnerability to masculine overtures. What makes it so hard for a girl to grow up with a gay father is that she never gets to see him loving, honoring, or protecting the women in his life. I was shocked in the person of Dr. Blair to behold a man who had power and influence and yet remained so humble, and so committed to helping others. Here was a man who identified with suffering and didn't run away from it, who was single and wasn't on the make.

In this giddy flood of unleashed emotions, I felt as though something cold and hard at my core was being melted away. It took me a while to get my bearings, and I soon recognized, with great misgiving, that I had very strong feelings for Dr. Blair personally.

An innate sense of my feminine being was starting to bloom after being abused and rejected for so many years.

In one of our earlier meetings, I could see that Dr. Blair assumed I had led a promiscuous life. Certainly that is usually the pattern with daughters who grow up in homes as sexually chaotic as mine had been. Intermittent and inconsistent as it may have been, it was only my Christian faith that had held me back from sliding into such a life.

I knew that my sexuality was being rightly aligned and was coming fully alive because I found particular qualities in Dr. Blair so overpoweringly attractive. His natural, masculine presence and his nonsexual interest in me were breaking through every obstruction from my childhood and pulling out the buried female desires within me. I'd never freely expressed such feelings before in my life—not even with Vince. We often marry someone who is only as intimate as we can bear to be at the time, someone who isn't going to threaten us in any way. That was the necessary sanctuary I had sought and found in the infinitely patient and supportive Vince. But now in my thirtieth year, I didn't want sanctuary and shelter anymore. I was luxuriating for the first time in my life to the full ripeness of my own womanhood and longed to respond in an unguardedly passionate way with a man. But the man who was calling all these primal urges out of me wasn't my husband; he was my shrink. As exciting and liberating as this transformation was, I didn't know how to proceed or how to be platonic and professional about all this. I didn't want to have an affair with my therapist, and there was no reason to believe Dr. Blair wanted one either. It was great to be so emotionally alive but distressing to feel that I was emotionally acting out at the level of an eight-year-old girl who's just seen her first Cary Grant movie.

I called a special meeting with Dr. Blair to discuss my concerns. I realize now with a twinge of embarrassment that he knew perfectly well what was going on. This process of transference I was going through—projecting all the positive feelings of my awakening onto the therapist who had overseen that awakening—is not at all uncommon. A patient is terribly vulnerable and open to manipulation at such a time. If at this time the psychiatrist is less than professional or perhaps returns some of the attraction that his patient is feeling, horrible abuses can and sometimes do take place.

After exchanging our greetings, I sat on the couch, and Dr. Blair looked at me for a long moment without saying a word, wearing an expression of kindness and vague amusement on his face. He seemed to be thinking something over and then abruptly got up, took a small pair of scissors from his desk, and went out to rummage about in his garden. He moved about from plant to bush to tree, inspecting and selecting the most perfect flowers, carefully cutting each one away from their stems. As he gathered these blossoms, he held each one up for a moment to the sunlight and turned it around, making sure it was unblemished.

This was pretty unusual behavior, but I can't say I was alarmed or even confused by his actions. I loved watching him out there. He seemed less like a doctor and more like a man—somehow older and frailer and even more sensitive than the man I'd come to know. In some way, I intuitively understood that what was going on was still therapy of some kind, but we had moved it off the doctor-patient level to a sub-verbal or even archetypal level. This was more like dance than analysis.

Dr. Blair returned after a few minutes with a loose handful of flowers that he took through to an adjoining room. A short minute later, he re-emerged with three flowers artfully arranged in a simple glass vase that he carefully set on the table beside me. This beautiful gesture struck me so deeply, I blurted out without thinking: "You know how to affirm femininity and womanhood! Don't you?"

His demeanor was calm, relaxed, almost playful. He went over and sat in his own chair, cradling the back of his head in clasped hands. There was no need for him to say anything more; it was spelled out there in his gesture. As a man, Dr. Blair had paid tribute to me as a woman. But he was not my man as I was not his woman, and so we both sat in our separate chairs. Before therapy, being a woman was like acting out a role for me, like being a person who just happened to live in a female body. Now I had come to under-stand that my personhood and my femininity were intimately and inextricably connected: Being a woman is part of who I am. Once my awareness of my own femininity was asserted and I could feel my need for intimacy increasing, I knew the greatest part of my work with Dr. Blair was done. Almost immediately, I began to deeply desire children for the first time. And I knew I wanted those children with Vince.

Another fearful bit of symmetry didn't occur to me until long after therapy. I was reflecting back on Dr. Blair's simple, and for me essential, gift of a few flowers in a glass vase and how much that signified for me in terms of taking full ownership of who I am as a person and a woman. And then, I remembered those watercolor paintings on the wall of my dad's bedroom of a few long-stemmed flowers in a glass vase that I utterly destroyed in a fury of frustra-tion at a father who could never affirm who I essentially am.

While I could have stuck with therapy longer, I felt the main work was done and it was time to get out—in fact, that God wanted me out. As much good as these meetings had accomplished, I knew they had become too central in my life. Though he respected boundaries absolutely, I knew I was too emotionally attached to Dr. Blair. I felt, in the main, that there was nothing more I could have processed at that time without substantially repeating myself, and emotionally I knew I was in danger of going over into the inappropriate zone. My mind, emotions, and will were all responding in a new and positive way to masculinity. Now, it was time to take my projections back from Dr. Blair and work this stuff out with the man I had married.

Epilogue

I've only met with my brothers a handful of times since Mom died, and we haven't exchanged words of any kind for more than three years now. After initiating many phone calls over the last few decades, and finding my brothers rarely returned the favor, I've decided to leave it in their court for a while and see if anything improves. I know that it was only my work in therapy and my faith that enabled me to get out from under the wreckage of our profoundly disordered home and live a decent, fully conscious life. I have been able to do this in a way that they never have. Vince suspects—and I suspect he may be right—that my faith in Christ and my willingness to undergo therapy have made my brothers uncomfortable and have probably contributed to the distance between my brothers and me.

Scott doesn't sympathize with me nor grasp my purposes for writing this book, likely because he was much younger and intentionally avoided as much of our home life as possible, preferring to conceal whatever family secrets of which he was aware and only choosing to reflect the brighter side. In an impulsive burst of fraternal solidarity, Thomas actually sent me a letter of encouragement and support just before I presented a brief to a Canadian Senate Committee as they deliberated on adding sexual orientation as a protective category under hate crime legislation. While his subsequent silence has been just as total as Scott's and I could not in all honesty describe my relationship with either brother as close, I continue to love them both and live in the hope that someday we will be more to each other than we are today.

Through occasional visits and letters and numerous phone calls, I achieved a good measure of forgiveness and peace in my relationship with Mom by the time she died at the age of sixty-seven from complications of the diabetes she'd struggled with all her life. I made the first overture by admitting to her that for all I'd doubted the wisdom of her racing into marriage with Al, he had slowly won me over. As part of my general mistrust of men as a species, I had misjudged Al at first, fearing he was just marrying Mom for her money. In fact, he was unfailingly kind, attentive, and supportive of her during the thirteen years of their marriage and unflinchingly saw her through the pains, disappointments, and indignities of declining health. I also came to recognize that being the age they were and having such a limited time together, it perhaps wasn't necessary that Mom fill Al in on all the gruesome details of her life with Dad. There was precious little he ever could have done to fix that anyway. What he could do—and did, God bless him—was round out my mother's life with a final chapter in which she was cherished as a woman and loved with a constancy she never previously had known.

Six months before she died, Mom reciprocated my healing gesture by calling me to ask for my forgiveness regarding Vince. Caught up in the same materialist worldview as my father and my brothers, she had spoken ill of him for years, putting him down as an inadequate provider. "Your husband is a good and moral man," she told me. "And that's what really matters."

Al called to tell me that Mom had died just a few days after I had weaned our second child. It was just after Thanksgiving 2001, almost ten years to the day after Dad's death. On my trip home from the funeral in Florida, at times the sun's rays hit the wing of the plane with such force that I couldn't look out the window. Closing my eyes in prayer and reflection, I realized there must be some sort of message in the timing of my parents' deaths. Was I supposed to be thankful for both of my parents—and for life itself—no matter how painful and confusing my early life with them had been? I was starting to come around to that conviction after having given birth to a son and a daughter of my own.

The home Vince and I were providing for our children was very different from the home in which I'd grown up, and I was coming to accept that God must have chosen my parents for a reason. It was my Christian duty to learn something important from all the misery and chaos of my early life and share my hard-won insights with the world. My parents were gone now. Though I would remain very much involved with the raising and teaching of our children for decades yet, the years of infancy were past. Both our kids were on their way.

Flying home through those blinding, dazzling clouds in the fall of 2001, hovering in the air for a few quiet moments between the world I was born into and the world I'd created with Vince, I realized that though the past cannot be changed, the future shines brightly, and with my faith to guide me and my family beside me, I would face whatever lay ahead with courage and grace.

Afterword

We have now come to the end of Dawn's story. Perhaps she will in the future provide us with further accounts of her life or perspectives on her family experiences, but for now we would like to offer our appreciation for her willingness to be so open and vulnerable in sharing material so deeply personal. We hope that her honesty will inspire and encourage others to share their stories as well. For those who were intrigued by her revelations and would like to find out more about Dawn, we would suggest visiting her website: www.dawnstefanowicz.com, where you can read additional brief accounts of other adults who grew up in similar households.

About the Author

Dawn Stefanowicz empathizes with those who struggle with sexual confusion, yet realizes how important it is—for us, for our children, and for lawmakers—to make the right choices when it comes to the issue of human sexuality. Raised in an "alternative" household with a homosexual father, his partners, and a passive mom, she affirms that children *are* powerfully impacted long-term by their family structures, their living arrangements, and the rules that govern their home and neighboring environments. Even in the midst of her childhood conflict and chaos, Dawn had intense courage to not only survive her situation, but learn life lessons in the midst of such overwhelming confusion. Now, she has a purpose to share her insights with the world.

Since the death of her father from AIDS in 1991 and the passing of her mother ten years later, Dawn realizes that none of her father's many partners are alive today either. She's become a candid media spokesperson on legislation that affects the safety and emotional health of children. Though she loved her dad, and later heard his many regrets, she gently shares her moments of joy, along with her travails, pain, fear, and confusion about early exposure to sexual activities and childhood sexual abuse in a manner that will broaden the understanding of the reader.

Dawn Stefanowicz is a published author, conference speaker, licensed accountant, and home educator living in London, Canada. Now married for twenty-three years, she and her husband have two children and are active in their church and community. Through involvement on professional boards and before Canadian and U.S. legislators, she has advocated for the needs of children, families, and society on public issues of sexuality, sharing the message contained in her published articles: "The Sad Side of Gay Parenting" (Mercatornet, 2007), "Life with a Gay Father: My Story" (NARTH, 2007), and "Same-Sex Marriage: Have the Best Interests of Children Been Considered?" (Agape Press, 2005).

Traumatic visual imprints and the dark secrets lurking just below the surface in a homosexual home left Dawn overwhelmingly confused, agonized, and impacted long-term as male roommates began to reside in her home shortly after her birth. In her first book, *Out from Under: The Impact of Homosexual Parenting,* she describes her disturbing experiences and the ripple effect of adult choices, high-risk sexual behaviors, and multiple partners being paraded before her in the home. Two decades of direct exposure to these stressful experiences in the home and the subcultures caused her desperate emotions, nightmares, and sexual confusion as she struggled with the impact of homosexuality. Despite all, however, Dawn lovingly reached out to her father as lifestyle choices caught up with him—then sought her own healing so she could provide a service to children like herself, who are, as she was, often too fearful to speak up for themselves.

For more information, please see the website http://www.dawnstefanowicz.com.

Endnotes

1. Unless otherwise noted, all Scriptures are taken from the King James Version of the Bible.

2. Scripture references marked NIV are taken from the *Holy Bible, New International Version*®, NIV®. Copyright © 1973, 1978, 1984 by the International Bible Society. Used by permission of Zondervan. All rights reserved.